a celebration of HEIRLOOM VEGETABLES

a celebration of HEIRLOOM VEGETABLES

GROWING AND COOKING OLD-TIME VARIETIES

Written and Illustrated by

ROGER YEPSEN

ARTISAN

New York

To Ali, who found both weeds and satisfaction behind the white picket fence

Designer: Pat Tan

Published in 1998 by Artisan,
a division of Workman Publishing Company, Inc.
708 Broadway
New York, NY 10003–9555

Printed in Singapore
10 9 8 7 6 5 4 3 2 1
First Printing

Library of Congress Cataloging-in-Publication Data

Yepsen, Roger B.
     A celebration of heirloom vegetables : growing and cooking
old-time varieties / Roger Yepsen.
             p.   cm.
     Includes index.
     ISBN 1-885183-88-7
     1. Vegetables—Heirloom varieties. 2. Vegetable gardening.
     3. Cookery (Vegetables)   I. Title.
SB324.73.Y46 1998
635—dc21   98-18278
                                 CIP

CONTENTS

LIVING ANTIQUES

As you rush to get through a day, the world often has to perform stunts to snare your attention. It might be a flame-colored warbler alighting on a nearby branch or an outrageous sunset becoming more lurid by the moment.

Or an heirloom vegetable. Through a funny name or odd appearance or intriguing taste, something as simple as a green ripe tomato can make us slow down and take notice. How is it that a dry bean the size of a fingernail acquired the grand name Cherokee Trail of Tears? Why would a parsnip, raised underground in Wisconsin, have the tropical scent of coconut about it? Are blue potatoes just a gimmick, or are they really something special to eat? Or, can that ripe green tomato taste very good?

This book is a gallery of living antiques. Many of them have been grown for

hundreds of years, and all survived because something about them caused people to continue putting seeds in the ground, season after season. Over their long histories, they've gone in and out of fashion. At the moment, old is in. Trend-conscious restaurants have become a beachhead for heirloom vegetables. Where once you'd order side dishes of a salad and baked potato, the menu might offer Brune d'Hiver (a cold-hardy French lettuce from the 1850s) and oven-roasted Anna Cheeka's Ozette fingerling potatoes (part of the booty that Spanish explorers brought back from the Andes). Even bean soups have gone varietal, celebrating such old-time favorites as Molasses Face and Swedish Brown Baking.

As yet we have no gardening DAR to certify which vegetables are heirlooms and which are arrivistes. The lines have been drawn at fifty years ago, at 1940, and at 1900. Even if an appropriate cut-off year could be agreed upon, the origins of many heirlooms

commercial varieties rather than tinker with those developed over the centuries for small-scale growers.

The old-time seeds languished in jars and envelopes. Many varieties died out, along with a generation of growers for whom saving seed each year was a way of life.

BUT DOES IT TASTE BETTER?

It would be simplest to say, sometimes yes, sometimes no. But that's a wishy-washy answer to a flawed question. The problem is the word "better." Even if it were possible to objectively determine the best-tasting tomato, would we want to resign ourselves to seeing nothing but that variety on our plates?

Clearly, people like a range of choices. That's why a catalog of heirlooms and oddities, *Seed Savers Yearbook*, currently offers eleven thousand varieties grown by gardeners around the world. The yearbook is published by the best-known North American grass roots organization, Seed Savers Exchange (along with a catalog for fruits, nuts, and berries, and another for heirloom flowers and herbs). Turn to the tomato section of the yearbook, and you find listings for 393 yellow and orange tomatoes alone. Compare that with perhaps a couple in a mainstream seed catalog, and none whatsoever at the supermarket. Are all 393 superior to a modern, mass-market yellow-orange variety? Not likely. But the world would be a poorer place without such golden gems as Azoychka, a Russian tomato with a citrusy flavor; Djena Lee's Golden Girl, a great-tasting heirloom from the garden of a Minnesota woman; and Striped German, which reveals

are hazy. Some of the best-known varieties were birthed in someone's backyard and acquired names and reputations only years later. Others are from abroad, and their ages can only be guessed at. Perhaps an elastic definition is best—one that expands to include both regional favorites and varieties with uncertain histories from other countries.

The entire notion of heirloom vegetables might never have come up if the past century had not seen a revolution in the way food is grown. In the interests of productivity, agricultural agencies developed varieties for large-scale growers—high-yielding vegetables and fruits suited to mechanical harvesting, intensive fertilizing, chemical pest and disease control, and the rigors of shipping to distant markets. At the same time, home gardening was shifting from a means of subsistence to a hobby, causing breeders to further concentrate on a red starlike pattern when sliced.

To begin sampling this bounty, you can browse the stands of market gardeners known for offering eye-catching and flavorful produce. Urban greengrocers may feature locally grown heirlooms. Many historic museums and farms have put in period gardens. But the best way to explore the thousands of celebrated and unsung heirlooms grown around the world is to grow your own.

Heirloom gardeners feel a connection with the long chain of growers before them. It takes many years to develop a variety by selection, and occasionally credit is given in the vegetable's name—Good Mother Stallard bean, Jimmy Nardello's sweet pepper, Nancy Hall sweet potato. Part of the joy of watching the tidy, compact bushes of McMahon's Texas Bird pepper ripen their fruits is a historical footnote: Thomas Jefferson also grew this variety from seed at Monticello. But the great majority of plant developers remain unknown to us. As you open the dry, brittle pods of the Vermont Cranberry bean and brightly hued seeds spill into your hand, you share the awe of anonymous New England farmers more than two centuries ago.

Heirloom gardeners also overlap with the lives of other cultures. The remarkable appearance of blue potatoes has made them the darlings of high-end greengrocers and chefs. But as you paw through the garden soil for the gemlike tubers, you are involved in an annual ritual that has sustained Peruvian Indians for uncounted centuries. A garden, then, can be an unusual sort of meeting place—a formalized rendezvous, right in your backyard, between you and other people and other times.

GARDENING WITH HEIRLOOMS

Not everyone who tucks into a bowl of Moon and Stars watermelon soup will care about the larger issues embraced by the heirloom movement. It may be enough to just acknowledge that the vegetables we drop into the shopping basket have varietal names and histories and that different regions have their own preferences. People in eastern Massachusetts march to a different rutabaga—Macomber—than the rest of the United States, where American Purple-Top Yellow is the norm. (Both are heirlooms, by the way, although you seldom see their names displayed in the store.)

You may be fortunate in having a nearby market that specializes in older varieties, but to really explore them you'll have to grow your own. Part of the fun is sleuthing sources of seeds. Like recent converts to any interest, heirloom growers like to talk shop, whether in person or by letter, phone, E-mail, and chatty notes printed in catalogs. A common question is, "What's new?" Which, to an heirloom enthusiast, means "What's new that's old?" Your garden will be host to plants from other climates and other cultures. The English are devoted to their parsnips; the Italians have their chicories; the French, their lettuces; the Chinese, various permutations of the cabbage; the Native Americans, beans, squash, and corn. It can be fascinating to grow these international favorites and then try them in recipes from the country of origin.

To get a start, you might begin by visiting local nurseries that have a reputation for offering unusual seedlings. (Nursery professionals in Agway caps and shop aprons have been known to catch the heirloom bug.) Another way to find local growers is to attend celebrations with a historic theme, craft fairs, and ethnic days. Farmers' markets and roadside stands may also lead you to heirloom growers with plants to sell. But for an unlimited selection of varieties, look to your mail box. The source listing at the end of this book includes gardeners' seed-saving organizations and companies devoting at least a portion of their catalogs to old-time varieties.

SAVING SEEDS

A complication in growing heirlooms is that many varieties have disappeared from the world's inventory, and continue to do so.

Seeds look about as perishable as sand and pebbles, and yet they are living objects—breathing, consuming their store of energy, and putting off tiny amounts of body heat—and as such they will perish in time. National seed banks are entrusted with preserving genetic material for the future, but their efforts tend to be spotty. That's why gardeners get into the habit of saving seeds. It's an international movement you can join with nothing but a shovel, a packet of seeds, and good intentions.

Hundreds of threatened varieties hang on from year to year only by the graces of amateur growers who stick seeds in the ground each spring and then go through the bother of collecting fresher seeds a few months later. Consider that if no one sows a particular variety for a few years, all of that low-tech genetic engineering

will be irrevocably lost. Wiping out a once-treasured soup bean is a quiet, passive act, unlike driving a grader through a rain forest.

There are less ideological reasons for saving seeds, of course. First, you stand to save money: Devoted gardeners may grow fifty or a hundred varieties a season, and all of those little packets add up. Another practical motive is that varieties come and go so quickly from commercial catalogs. The melon you loved last year may be unavailable this spring—unless you thought to scoop out and dry a supply of seeds.

Seed savers also know that a good variety can get even better if they save its seeds from year to year. This works in a couple of ways. Plants may gradually adapt to their environmental niche, genetically programming themselves to handle such challenges as insufficient rainfall or a short growing season. And you can guide the plant's own genetic research-and-development. This is the sexual business of cross-pollination, through which variations come about—tall or short, colorful or drab, slow or quick to mature, sweet or tart, and so on. Generations of farmers have saved seeds from those

plants that showed promising traits. A cold-climate grower might choose to propagate seeds from an okra that ripened a few days early. Another might select for a milder-flavored chicory or a shorter bean plant that wouldn't need to scale a trellis. Through a backyard sort of Darwinism, different versions of the same vegetable come about, and the best are given names. This process can seem painstakingly slow—it's thought to take at least five generations for a sought-after quality to "stick" in the seeds.

Not all vegetables go about the Birds and the Bees in the same way. Most exchange pollen between flowers of their own kind, in something vaguely analogous to animal reproduction. Certain vegetables are less particular about partners and will mate, or cross, with other plants in the same broad genus; others stick to their own species. And then there are the self-pollinators that usually take care of everything right within the blossom.

Every generation presents new players, each with variations that might catch the grower's eye. Most new wrinkles are just wrinkles, and nothing special. And any improvements are apt to be incremental. But occasionally a "sport," as genetic exceptions are called, has great promise. The most-cherished wine grape, Cabernet Sauvignon, is thought to have spontaneously sprouted as a wild vine in France before the Revolution; its surname even means "wild." In the garden, determinate tomatoes—the ones that restrain themselves to a bushlike form rather than sprawling—all descend from a prim sport that appeared on a Florida farm in 1914.

Plants have reproduced by swapping pollen ever since they first made blossoms. But as natural as this open-pollination process may seem, it's something of an endangered antique itself. An ever-larger share of the seed market is going to vegetables of a very different sort.

THE HYBRID CONTROVERSY

Any discussion of seed saving would be incomplete without mentioning hybrid varieties. These plants yield seeds that don't work.

Some hybrid seeds are as sterile as pocket lint, while others produce offspring that don't look like the parent and will almost certainly be inferior to it. And yet, since World War II, major seed producers have shifted the bulk of their offerings from traditional open-pollinated varieties to hybrids.

A hybrid is a variety developed through a sophisticated process that begins by inbreeding open-pollinated plants over a number of generations. The offspring are weak or malformed and of no use. But the goal is to arrive at a generation of plants that are genetically stable and identical with one another. These inbred lines are then crossed repeatedly with one another, as the breeders look for certain characteristics in their progeny. Over time, they can program just about anything they want into a vegetable—color, disease resistance, firmness when ripe.

Hybrids tend to be highly productive, a quality called hybrid vigor; they are uniform; and they typically ripen within a short period, making automated harvesting easier. These are advantages to a large-scale commercial grower, and most new varieties are bred with them in mind.

So, what's wrong with having highly trained experts design super-vegetables for us? That's a question apt to raise hackles. For a person who gardens with the notion of self-reliance, it can be galling to think of the marketplace being taken over by varieties that lack the ability to reproduce themselves. This may be the ultimate expression of a throwaway society—throwaway, one-time-use seeds. Another point of contention is that hybridizers tend to overlook the special needs of the gardener, who is less concerned with the logistics of harvest and shipping than with growing something great to eat.

It should be pointed out that agribusiness wouldn't be happy with traditional varieties. For example, the open-pollinated Brandywine tomato is often said to be the finest of them all, with a rich, complex, consummately tomatoey flavor. But this beloved heirloom tends to bruise and deteriorate easily, and Ohio market gardener Jerry Moomey explains that's why you seldom see America's best tomato in produce departments. It's even a challenge for him to take boxes of Brandywines to a farmers' market for sale the same day. But a gardener will have no problem walking across the yard with them.

This issue goes beyond a clash between gardeners and large-scale agriculture, however. As hybrids threaten to displace open-pollinated varieties from the market, a long view suggests that we are in danger of squandering our rich genetic heritage—and its promise of better flavor, enhanced nutritional value, and adaptability in the face of disease outbreaks and global climatic changes. In much the same way, scientists warn that in allowing the plant's species to become extinct, we are depleting the trove of genetic material from which

miraculous new medicines might one day be developed.

And so it is with a sense of mission that an heirloom gardener will keep thirty or a hundred varieties alive through the only means available—planting seeds and gathering seeds. "Backyard gardeners are emerging as the most vitally concerned stewards of this irreplaceable genetic wealth," writes Seed Savers Exchange director Kent Whealy, "and we must quickly accept our responsibility." Small-scale seed houses continue to offer broad choices of open-pollinated seeds, when it would be far easier to stock only the Big Boys and Slice Master. Judy Gaunt of Terra Edibles, an Ontario seed company, writes in her catalog, "Since many of the seeds offered here are unavailable commercially or difficult to find, I would encourage you to try saving your own seeds from them." Phipps Country Store and Farm, a family company offering many unusual bean varieties, asks customers to send in samples of family heirloom beans for testing on the chance of coming up with new varieties. Johnny's Selected Seeds, one of the most visible of the companies offering heirlooms, offers a rotating selection of varieties to nudge gardeners into the habit of saving their own seeds.

STARTING PLANTS FROM SEEDS

There is something reassuring about the spring ritual of buying seedlings from a nursery. You're off to a galloping head start, without having to squint to read seed packets, prepare potting soil, or monkey around with fluorescent lights. And it can be daunting to look at those flats with their green wisps of life, knowing that one wrong move will have the seedlings drooping their little heads and giving up.

Nevertheless, growing vegetables from seed is not all that challenging. All you need is a catalog with good, explicit directions—Johnny's sets the standard— and an aptitude for putting up with the seedlings' crotchety requirements for moisture, light, and odd combinations of warm and cool temperatures. Most supplies—flats, pots, soil-less medium, fertilizers, lights—should be available locally. If not, you can order them by mail through the larger catalogs.

It's easy to lose track of which seedlings ended up where as you shuttle them from flats to pots to bigger pots to the garden. Unless you have an outstanding memory for such things, you'll be well served by a waterproof marker, pot labels, and larger plant labels for the beds. Once plants are set out in the garden, you might want to back up the labels with a map; labels have a way of disappearing, especially if there are any squashes in the vicinity.

SUMMER STRETCHERS

As gardeners gain experience, they tend to become impatient with the length of the growing season. There are two basic strategies for dealing with that.

You can raise soil temperatures in spring by laying down black plastic mulch. Later, to help hold in warmth invested in the soil, use row covers of plastic or fabric. Catalogs offer well-thought-out cover systems, but in a pinch you can ward off frosts with a simpler, if less elegant, alternative that costs nothing. Accumulate cardboard cartons over the summer, break them apart at the seams to flatten them, and store in the garage or basement. When overnight temperatures threaten fall crops, go out into the garden the evening before and cover the vegetables.

Another way to improve performance is to choose varieties suited to your climate. Unlike modern hybrids that are offered universally to wide markets, many older varieties are specialists. Seed catalogs may mention the strengths and limitations of each. Terra Edibles lists tomatoes that it judges will do well for northern gardeners. "Developed by a Quebec plant breeder," says the description for one variety. Another blurb reads, "Offered especially for those in the Maritimes." Southern Exposure Seed Exchange of Virginia focuses on varieties that should succeed well in the Mid-Atlantic region, characterized by "high summer heat, humidity, numerous plant diseases, uneven precipitation, and occasional high temperatures in the early spring and late fall." It may also be helpful to read gardeners' comments under the entries for each variety in the annual *Seed Savers Yearbook*. "Didn't work for me here," and, "Got flowers but not a single melon," are examples of the over-the-fence garden gossip that can guide you in finding the best variety for your site.

Come September, gardens are apt to have something in common with public swimming pools—they're empty, even when the weather is fine. And yet many vegetables, both greens and root crops, taste better when challenged by fall's cooler temperatures and shorter days. To take advantage of a second, late-season crop of cool-weather varieties, you have to remember to sow them in midsummer, when most gardeners are preoccupied by tomatoes and peppers and corn. You can start seeds in pots set out in a cooler part of the yard; this strategy has the added benefit of allowing you to grow two crops at once, so that you're ready to tuck in the fall vegetables as you yank the exhausted summer plants.

IN THE KITCHEN

The better the vegetable, the simpler its preparation can be. You can employ a smaller cast of supporting ingredients, few if any herbs and spices—and forget about smothering sauces.

All too often, recipes treat vegetables as neutral blotters for the grosser delights—salt and sugar, fat and oil. Just as American fast-food pizza uses the crust as an edible plate on which to pile cheese and meat, vegetables are humbled as vehicles for butter, cream, and cheese or as side acts for the meaty main event. Mistreatment of vegetables isn't anything new; for more than a century, cookbooks and magazines have directed us to overcook, oversalt, and oversauce. In the process, nuances of flavor, aroma, and texture are lost. When we eulogize the cooking of our grandmothers and great aunts, chances are we aren't talking about their flair with vegetables.

If you take the trouble either to grow or to shop for first-rate produce, then flatter it by steaming or sautéing lightly and dressing with a drizzle of olive oil and vinegar. Feel free to let a single vegetable shine as a side dish. It's become traditional to combine vegetables, as if a solo performance would be risky. Many of us grew up with some version of succotash, chow-chow, or slumgullion—long-simmering dishes that tend to taste as frumpy and out-of-date as they sound. If these mélanges are old family favorites of yours, continue to honor them; but you might consider that fine vegetables, like fine wine grape varieties, are worth savoring by themselves rather than in corner-smoothing blends. Ornate casseroles, you might say, are the jug wines of vegetable gardening.

Tomatoes, as perhaps the best-loved of heirlooms, invite us to become connoisseurs. They offer an almost limitless repertoire of colors, shapes, sizes, and tastes among their thousand-plus varieties. And even so rustic a crop as rutabagas has among its limited membership (just twenty-four commercial varieties and thirty-six through Seed Savers Exchange) a range of virtues worth investigating. This great diversity comes as news to most of us, having been numbed by the anonymity of supermarket produce departments—you can have six flavors of Quaker Instant Grits, but only one unnamed red tomato, one unnamed snap bean, and so on.

A sad result is that when market gardeners offer something out of the ordinary, customers sometimes shun it the way earlier centuries did eggplants and tomatoes. Lowell Seip, a Pennsylvania grower, recently discovered the cherry tomato of his dreams after years of testing and was stunned when it sat untouched at the family's roadside stand. It was some time before he realized that, because the tomato was orange, people assumed it was unripe. Even after offering free samples, he was unable to sell more than a few boxes. When Washington State grower Douglas Hendrickson presented customers with a salad mix that included kale, Asian greens, chard, and wild mustards, a common response was, "Where's the lettuce?" He now hands out flyers introducing the odder items, with recipes to help people get acquainted with them.

We all have our comfort foods, but narrow-minded taste buds are no better than any other kind of provincialism. Americans have earned an international reputation for preferring bland, sweet food and beverages. That said, we are becoming more discriminating. The shift may have been spurred when American wineries began marketing varietals—that is, wines named for the dominant grape. Next, microbreweries trumpeted their regionalism with funky-sounding regionalized products—a radical departure from the national brewers' devotion to uniformity. Bars now proudly display shelves of single-malt Scotch, brew their own beers, and have reintroduced varietal ciders—a bit of Americana that faded out in the 1800s. American bread was ripe for this sort of rehabilitation. Now we see bakeries displaying their so-called artisan loaves right out in the open (state health laws permitting) so that customers can appreciate the heft and crustiness.

KEEP IT SIMPLE

Not long ago, an American student at a Tuscan cooking school was shocked at the simplicity of the dishes under study. "Where are all the ingredients?" he asked himself. "Where's the garlic?"

Back home he observed that Americans were dropping the final vowel from Italian words but seemed to compensate by tagging inauthentic ingredients—fresh oregano, portobello mushrooms, raw garlic—onto every classical Italian recipe. Clichés clutter cooking just as they do speech, music, and art. We find ourselves seasoning reflexively: Italian means garlic, Chinese means sesame oil, Indian means curry powder, and so on.

At one time, American cooking was pared down in the extreme. An example is this recipe for Sautéed Parsnips, reprinted in its entirety from Fanny Farmer's *The Boston Cooking-School Cook Book* (1923): "Cut cold, boiled young parsnips in sixths, lengthwise. Sauté in butter until delicately browned and sprinkle with salt and pepper." No trendy spice-of-the-moment, no flavored oils. Minnesota seed saver Dorothy Beiswenger recalls, "Years ago a specific recipe wasn't always used by plain folk. Stew included any available vegetable. The true flavor of vegetables was sought after. No disguises were needed."

Try stripping ingredients from both cookbook recipes and your own old favorites, whenever they seem too boutique or too baroque. If your vegetables are harvested optimally and rushed into the kitchen, elaborate preparation may be as pointless as colorizing an old film noir.

ABOUT THE RECIPES

Most of the recipes in this book are presented in a conventional manner—every measurement and step spelled out. But, in the spirit of older cookbooks, some are only outlines and require improvisation. As with any creative craft, recipes are meant to be tampered with. By tampering, we gather confidence and, over time, can hope to arrive at something of a personal style.

If you feel stuck and uninspired—being responsible for two or three meals a day can chase away the culinary muse—experiment with an unfamiliar cooking utensil such as a generous-size wok, a Moroccan *tagine* pot, or a Mexican *olla*. You might also invite yourself into the kitchen of a friend who cooks innovatively or inveigle your way behind the swinging doors of a favorite restaurant. Looking over the shoulder of a cook with panache can be more stimulating than any cookbook.

These recipes assume that you'll rinse and inspect all vegetables before using them and that you'll use

fresh herbs and spices to season your fresh vegetables. The oil of choice is usually olive, but feel free to substitute (or experiment with) other oils: Mustard, almond, walnut, and light and dark sesame oils subtly shift the foundations of a dish in interesting ways. Years ago, cookbooks routinely specified vegetable and fruit varieties—an old Fanny Farmer recipe called for McLean peas (a variety that since has disappeared from cultivation)—but we've lost this sophistication. A few of the recipes that follow will name a certain variety, but you should not feel bound by the suggestion.

If you want to compare two or more varieties of a crop, make split recipes and invite family or friends to join you in a taste test—five chicories, two kohlrabis, a bouquet of lettuces, or whatever a trip to the garden happens to yield. Use colored toothpicks to keep track of what's what, and record comments in a gardening

journal. The exercise of describing tastes and aromas can also help you develop an informed palate.

The vegetable chapters give guidelines on harvesting for peak flavor and texture—and nutrition, although it goes without saying that tired-looking vegetables are apt to be anemic. It's not easy to pick vegetables at their very best, especially those like peas and snap beans that not only mature overnight but also practice protective coloration amidst their foliage. You have to be as vigilant with crops as you are with weeds.

Once vegetables have been picked, try to use them as soon as possible. It helps to be ready with a plan for the harvest—a recipe you're eager to try, such as a new twist on ratatouille just as the eggplants are ripening. When all signs point to a bumper crop of a certain vegetable, prepare by consulting books on putting up foods so that you can store that goodness for the months ahead. Freezing, canning, drying, and smoking are messy and time-consuming, but they allow you to extend the satisfactions of gardening until next year's seed catalogs start arriving in the mail.

Although processing food for storage can lower its quality and nutritional value, certain fresh vegetables are transformed into new, flavorful forms. A rich, slowly simmered tomato sauce is as sumptuous as the fresh fruit from which it is distilled. Dried chili peppers acquire overtones that are missing altogether when they are just picked. Several squash varieties and root crops actually improve in flavor with storage. And almost any garden produce can be turned into a juice, jelly, sauce, or chutney.

What to do if there's a surplus after both the family and the larder are full? In a more casual era, gardening publications suggested taking extras down to the corner grocer to barter for canned goods and flour. Lugging bags of homegrown produce into a supermarket would be all but unthinkable today. Instead, share your good fortune with friends who don't garden. Or pile the vegetables atop an overturned cardboard box on the front lawn along with a "free" sign. Old gardening books and magazines promoted another idea—bringing some of the harvest to people in the community who were less fortunate. That's an heirloom practice worth reviving.

THE VEGETABLES, A TO Z

The vegetables illustrated on the following pages are scruffy, personable, idiosyncratic models right out of the garden. No effort has been made to come up with an ideal, generalized composite of the variety. This means the vegetables you bring forth may bear only a family resemblance to the images you see here.

Beans are a true North American heirloom. They've been grown by Native Americans for thousands of years as one of the Three Sisters, along with squash and corn. Bean blossoms are self-pollinating, which suggests that some modern-day varieties are little changed from those grown long ago.

But beans aren't nearly as popular today as they once were. One reason may be the complexity surrounding the three stages of their life. We eat the immature green pods; less often, the fresh beans shelled from the pod; and finally, dry beans are reconstituted in boiling water.

BEANS

This makes a bean harder to understand than, say, a tomato or head of lettuce.

Although green beans are still a common side dish, supermarkets rarely offer shelled fresh beans. And to the cook who is unfamiliar with them, dry beans are apt to look unappealing, even unpalatable. *Joy of Cooking* once described them as a "dull" food.

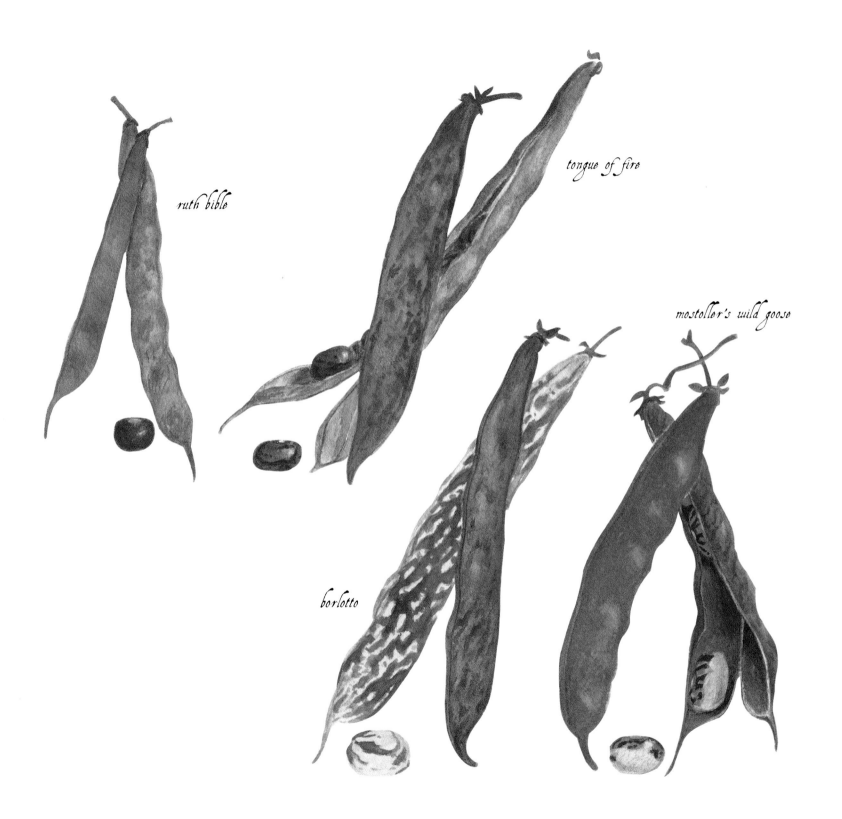

ruth bible

tongue of fire

mostoller's wild goose

borlotto

Then, in the 1970s, the decade that gave us the word *ecogourmet,* the bean went through a rehabilitation of sorts. Cookbooks hailed it as environmentally friendly, low on the food chain, and a vegetarian source of protein—all with a touch of Third World exotica. Recipes earnestly reported such statistics as this one from Beverly White's *Bean Cuisine* (Beacon Press, 1977): An acre of soybeans will support a human's life for just 77 days if used as feed and converted to meat, or 6.1 *years* if the human were to eat those beans directly.

Today's heirloom bean revival has its own agenda, of course, but taste also counts for a lot. North American cooks have dug deeper into the cuisines of other cultures, as well as our own bean-loving pockets in New England, southern Louisiana, and the Southwest. The vegetable that was good for the planet is now also good tasting.

For those who aren't conversant with bean lingo, here is a quick glossary. Immature pods are known as snap or string beans. A horticultural variety is one intended to be harvested at the middle stage, by removing the fully formed but soft seeds from the green pods; they're also known as shell (or shelly) beans. A dry or field bean may be of a variety considered best suited for dry use, but most can also be harvested at one or both of the younger stages.

To continue, a bush variety is one that will grow into a reasonably tidy plant, whereas a pole bean becomes long and meandering and needs the support of a wall, fence, trellis, or, obviously, pole. A wax bean is simply a variety with tender yellow pods. Lima, runner, and tepary beans form three other species. Limas, also known as butterbeans, produce seeds of the familiar wide, flat shape. Runners are known for their showy blossoms, and their use as a vegetable has gone in and out of fashion over the years. Tepary beans have been grown in the Southwest and Mexico since pre-Columbian times, but their preference for a hot, dry climate has restricted their cultivation.

Beans are a hit with heirloom gardeners. They have pedigree. They are beautiful, like tiny and highly burnished works of abstract art (although people read faces and such in the patterns, as they do in the moon). Beans have great nutritional credentials. And they aren't hard to grow.

GROWING

Beans are planted directly in the garden once the soil has warmed to at least 65 degrees F. Set bush-type beans 1 inch deep and 2 inches apart in rows spaced 24 to 36 inches. Pole beans trained to a wire or trellis should be set 1 inch deep and 3 inches apart, in rows at least 36 inches apart; if you are using poles, plant six to eight seeds to each pole, thinning to the four strongest plants. Lima varieties need a head start in northern gardens, or the beans may not have time to fully form; set seeds indoors around the expected last frost date.

Most of the bean heirlooms you'll find are bush varieties, meaning that they grow into reasonably compact bushes. Pole beans are often bypassed by gardeners leery of having to bother with supporting the plants. But pole varieties bear over a longer period, meaning less danger of a bean glut. And their vertical growth takes up less precious garden space.

The easiest way to get pole beans aloft is planting them along a wall or fence. Failing those resources, pound metal fencing posts or wooden stakes at intervals along the rows and run horizontal wires along the top and about a foot from the bottom. Finally, run vertical lengths of twine between these wires, spacing them every 6 inches or so; these will serve as ladders for the plants as they reach for the heavens.

HARVESTING

For string beans, you have to be vigilant. Within a day they go from tender to tough. Harvest them young, when not much more than three quarters of the full size stated in catalogs and gardening books; the seeds within should still be small. Keep picking regularly to encourage a greater yield. Note that bush beans tend to be ready for harvest at least a week earlier than pole varieties.

For shell beans and limas, the seeds should be fully formed but still green and soft to the touch. For dry varieties, allow the beans to harden in the pods; they are ready to be brought under cover to complete their drying when your thumbnail leaves only a slight dent. Pull up the plants by the roots and store in the garage or an outbuilding. Harvest the fully hardened beans by whacking the plants around inside a large cardboard carton or by placing the plants inside a cloth bag and swinging the bag about.

SAVING SEEDS

Bean strains usually remain pure because plants are self-pollinating, but if you are serious about maintaining an heirloom, it should be kept a hundred feet away from other varieties. The exception is runner beans, which are more readily pollinated by bees; if you will be preserving an heirloom runner, grow just one variety per year. (By the way, beans are not good subjects for hybridizing because each flower ends up yielding only a small number of seeds; this is one reason many old varieties continue to be commercially available.) To gather the seeds, see the previous paragraph on harvesting dry beans.

Although dry beans look as immutable as pebbles, they in fact are breathing, metabolizing organisms. As such they have a finite life span, and to preserve a variety from extinction it must be grown at least every few years. Many gardeners across the continent have taken the responsibility for maintaining a few or several dozen bean varieties.

HORTICULTURAL

Borlotto. Known also as Borlotti (the Italian plural of Borlotto), this old Italian standard has found its way into the Portuguese repertoire as well. Harvest at any stage.

Mostoller's Wild Goose. Few vegetable varieties have inspired as much historical research as this one. In 1865, the story goes, a western Pennsylvania miller's wife, Sarah Mostoller, was cleaning a goose that her son had shot. She found several beans of an unfamiliar variety in the bird's distended crop. When the family planted them the following spring, the plentiful harvest made good baked beans and soup. Five generations later, the family continues to grow this pole variety.

And where did the unlucky goose harvest those special beans? The best guess is the nearby fields of Cornplanter Indians.

Use this variety young as a snap or shelling bean, or wait for the distinctively patterned beans to dry.

Ruth Bible. This bean is credited to the Bouys family of Kentucky in the 1830s. Plants are very productive.

Tongue of Fire. A bush variety from Tierra del Fuego, Tongue of Fire's dramatically decorated pods hold a versatile bean that's good for eating fresh as shellies, for canning, freezing, or drying. The pods will be among the first in the garden to dry.

SNAP BUSH

Bountiful. Sow in early June and late July for two crops of this fast-growing variety. They yield a good harvest, and take well to freezing.

Fin des Bagnols. This has long been a favorite filet bean. It is ready to pick a few days before standard snaps. Beans should be harvested daily to ensure tenderness.

Low's Champion. Also seen listed as a dry bean, Low's is especially popular with heirloom growers. It comes from New England and may have originated with Native Americans. Harvest as snaps or shellies, or dry these deep-red beans.

Magpie. The black-and-white seeds are said to resemble magpie birds. Pods are stringy unless harvested very young. Magpie was introduced by Sutton in 1909; it may have had an earlier origin in France.

Tendergreen Improved. The meaty pods are often used for canning and freezing. Tendergreen continues to perform as the weather heats up.

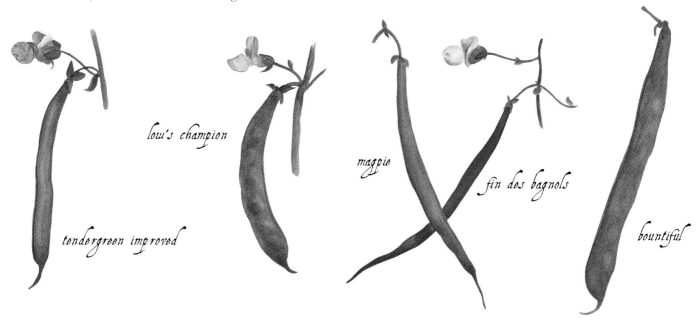

low's champion

tendergreen improved

magpie

fin des bagnols

bountiful

DRY BUSH

Agassiz Pinto. Expect this pinto to yield dry beans a few days earlier than other pintos. The dry beans have an especially good texture when cooked.

Andrew Kent. Northeastern gardeners know this Maine heirloom as a soup bean, but it can also be harvested as a shelly.

Black Coco. Use Black Cocos as snap beans, shellies, or dry beans. As dry beans, they take less time in the pot than most. They're often chosen in the Southwest for refried beans.

Black Valentine. Black Valentine dates to the first half of the nineteenth century, and E.L.D. Seymour recommended it as the best bush bean for gardeners in his 1914 how-to book, *Garden Profits*. Judging by the number of gardeners offering Black Valentine in the *Seed Savers Yearbook*, the bean remains an exceptionally interesting variety. Pick them as snaps and shellies and take advantage of their marked flavor when dry in soups.

Blue Speckled Tepary. The teparies make up another species of bean, grown for centuries in the Southwest and Mexico. Over the years, various Native American settlements—one on an island in the Sea of Cortés, others on mile-high plateaus—came up with their own varieties, and these are just now coming to the attention of the rest of the continent. This bluish tepary is from the southern Mexican highlands. As with others of the species, it is delicately patterned and

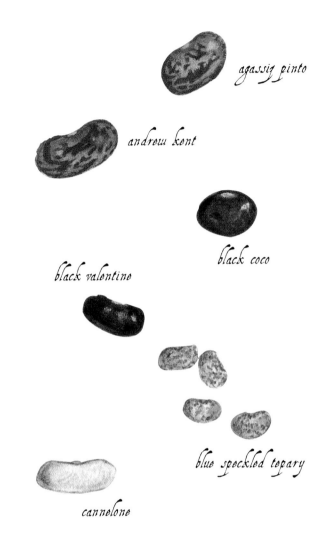

agassiz pinto

andrew kent

black coco

black valentine

blue speckled tepary

cannelone

has its own attractive scent and flavor. Serve the beans simply, with oil, vinegar, and a bit of salt. They're too fine to burden with molasses and smoked ham.

Cannelone. Look familiar? This is the white bean you find in many Italian recipes, minestrone among them. Cannelone (or Cannellini) has been grown since the 1800s. The beans have a rich, meaty flavor and are good for baking as well as soups.

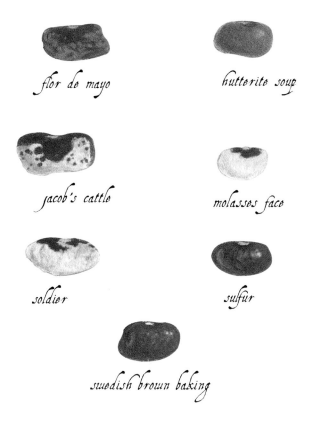

flor de mayo

hutterite soup

jacob's cattle

molasses face

soldier

sulfur

swedish brown baking

Flor de Mayo. The colors of this old Mexican bean are variable, warming from pale purple to tan. The flavor of the beans when simmered is very mild, perhaps with a hint of smokiness.

Hutterite Soup. As the name suggests, this bean is most handy in soups, quickly cooking into a particularly creamy consistency. It was brought to North America in the 1700s by the communal Hutterite sect of Anabaptists.

Jacob's Cattle. Harvest these beans as snaps and for shelling or wait to use them dry—they're a favorite for baking, with an excellent taste that strikes some people as similar to potatoes and others like molasses. This New England bean takes its name from the Biblical story of Jacob and the spotted cattle; alternate names include Dalmation and Trout. It's a good choice for growing in cooler zones.

Molasses Face. So called for the brown pattern around the eye. Known also as Maine Yellow Eye, these beans are commonly used for baking in that state. The flavor can taste green, or grassy.

Soldier. Use your imagination, and the pattern around the eye turns into a soldier. New England knows its baking beans, and this is one of that region's best.

Sulfur. This southern variety, a.k.a. Brimstone and Golden Cranberry, may predate the Civil War. The beans can be enjoyed as snaps. The dry beans are known for producing a vegetarian "gravy" when simmered or baked.

Swedish Brown Baking. Try this nutty-flavored variety as baked beans or in soups; it makes a rich gravy as it cooks. As might be expected of a bean brought to North America by Swedish immigrants, plants perform well in cooler areas.

DRY POLE

Blue Coco. The name sounds like an oxymoron, but it refers to color only, not flavor. The pod is purplish blue, and the meaty-tasting beans within are chocolatey-hued. Blue Coco comes from eighteenth-century France.

Cherokee Trail of Tears. Folklore tends to attach itself to vegetables and, for some reason, to beans in particular. This variety was first grown by the Cherokees, then carried west in the 1800s when their lands in the Carolinas were usurped. The pods can be picked early as snaps.

Good Mother Stallard. This heirloom is a good soup bean, available only through seed-saving networks.

Hopi Red Lima. Limas are a species unto themselves and are often listed apart from other beans in catalogs. Hopi Red sounds like the legacy of the ancients, but in fact it was developed not long ago by a Hopi artist, Fred Kabotie.

Hopi Yellow Lima. The Hopis use this bean in spring ceremonies, both as objects to attach to dolls, rattles, and bows and to cook into a soup for feasts.

Jackson Wonder Lima. This productive lima is said to date to 1888. Plants do well even in dry, hot conditions. Use the beans fresh or dry.

Lynch Butterbean. Some gardeners report identifying eight different patterns among their annual crops of this family heirloom; gardener Chris Inhulsen of Georgia says that children enjoy harvesting them to see what pops out of the pods. The variety is being kept alive by the efforts of backyard seed savers.

New Mexico Appaloosa. It is easy to sense that the arresting graphics of this heirloom are the

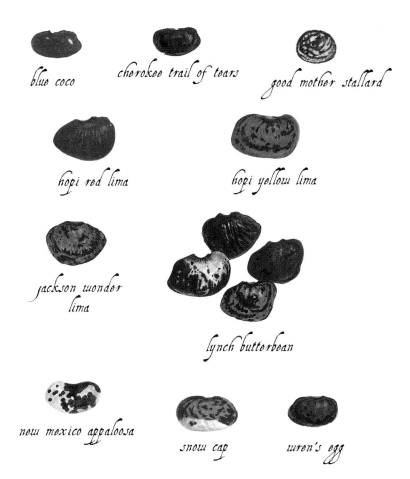

blue coco　　*cherokee trail of tears*　　*good mother stallard*

hopi red lima　　*hopi yellow lima*

jackson wonder lima

lynch butterbean

new mexico appaloosa　　*snow cap*　　*wren's egg*

expression of some sort of universal Bean Mind. On a mundane level, Appaloosas can be appreciated as snap beans, shellies, or dry beans.

Snow Cap. Snow Cap is one of those heirlooms pretty enough to put in a glass bowl and place on a windowsill as an art object or object of contemplation. The beans are mild in flavor and cook into a good soup.

Wren's Egg. Wren's Egg is suited to modest-size gardens because the plants occupy relatively little space. It should yield well until the end of the growing season. Use the beans as snaps or shellies.

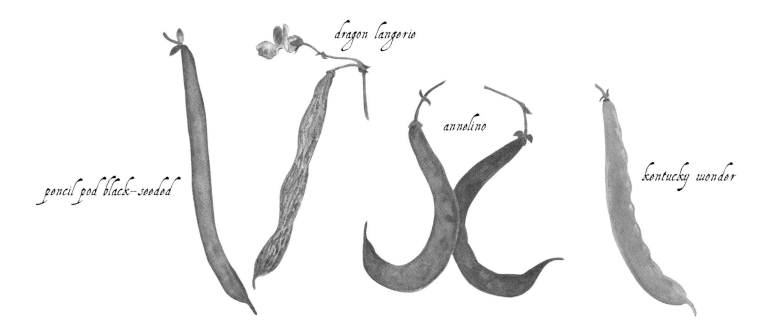

pencil pod black-seeded

dragon langerie

annelino

kentucky wonder

WAX

Annelino. Grow both colors of this Italian heirloom pole bean, yellow and green, and steam them together. Excellent flavor and a fishhook shape set them apart.

Dragon Langerie. You may find this one offered by supermarkets as Dragon Tongue. The appearance of the pods is striking and memorable. Flavor is very good as a snap bean, even if eaten raw. One seed company, Bountiful Gardens, notes that this bean is a favorite with its garden staff and a conversation piece besides.

Kentucky Wonder. Also known as Old Homestead. This highly popular bean produces good crops that can be picked as snaps or shellies.

Pencil Pod Black-Seeded. From jet black seeds come slim, bright yellow pods. The variety dates to around 1900. It was the work of western New York

breeder Calvin Keeney, called the Father of the Stringless Bean for his efforts (early varieties often had tough strings that needed to be removed before cooking). The fresh beans are tender and stringless, and they continue to appear on into the warm days of summer.

RUNNER

Black. When simmered, the glossy black beans have a rich taste that brings to mind comparisons ranging from wine to steak. They are often used by chefs for Southwestern cuisine.

Painted Lady. With origins traced to seventeenth-century Portugal, this runner may owe its survival in part to the added attraction of bi-color blossoms—the standards are red, the wings and keel are white. The fresh beans are good for freezing. Cooked, the dried beans taste remarkably like chestnuts.

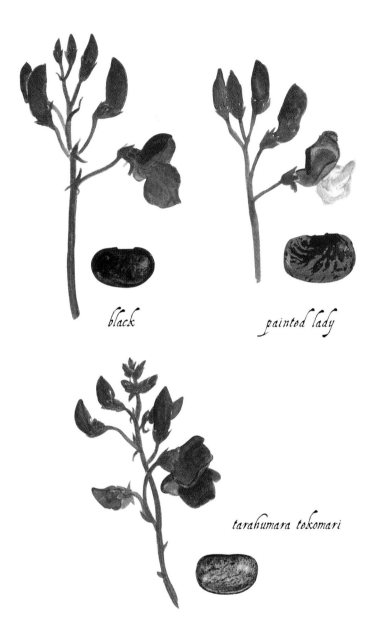

black

painted lady

tarahumara tekomari

Tarahumara Tekomari. These beans are from the Sierra Madre of Chihuahua, Mexico. The shiny beans are remarkably beautiful, all the more so for their quiet contrast to the poppy-bright blossoms that precede them. When cooked, they have a slight, pleasant edge to their nutty flavor.

BEAN COMPANIONS

While you're preparing to plant beans, consider buying seed for two easily grown herbs that have long been associated with them, summer savory and epazote. Summer savory can be used fresh or dried in bean dishes, and its presence in the garden has been credited with encouraging the growth of nearby beans. In acknowledgment of the association of these two plants, German markets offer green beans tied in bundles with a few sprigs of Bohnenkraut, or bean-leaf, as summer savory is known. Epazote is a curiously scented herb used in Mexican bean cuisine, for both flavor and its reputed powers as a digestive. In India, asafetida and ginger are used to spice bean dishes for the same reasons.

Bean Basics

To cook snap beans, cut off the ends and steam, simmer, or sauté until just tender; remember that beans will continue to cook by retained heat. Certain old-time varieties will have a tough string along the seam that should be removed before cooking. Shelly beans are popped from the shell, then cooked in the same ways as snaps.

Dry beans will cook faster if soaked beforehand. Begin by rinsing them well and removing any small stones masquerading as beans. Then put the beans in a bowl, cover with at least three times as much water, and cull any that float. Don't add the pinch of baking soda called for by many cookbooks. Soak them overnight, or from breakfast until dinnertime. (To speed this process, boil the beans for a couple of minutes in the water in which they'll soak.) They've soaked long enough when you halve a test bean and it is the same shade from center to skin. Drain beans after soaking to reduce the complex sugars that can cause gastric discomfort.

To cook dry beans, cover with plenty of water to ensure that they won't burn at the bottom of the pan, and replenish as necessary. Allow 1 to 2 hours of simmering time. To further cut down on complex sugars, drain the beans roughly halfway through this period and add fresh water. Beans are easier to digest when fully cooked. To check, remove a couple from the pot and blow on them; the skins should split and pull back.

Expect 1 cup of dry beans to yield from 2 to 2½ cups when cooked.

Baked Swedish Brown Beans

Serves 6 to 8

Many baked bean recipes lean heavily on salt and meat. That's because beans are popularly thought of as bland and characterless. This recipe lets the flavor of the heirloom bean come through. Despite the number of ingredients, the beans themselves are the star.

Swedish Brown beans have a sweet, clean scent as they simmer. Reserve some of the cooking water to add to the baking beans if they appear to be drying somewhat.

2 cups dry Swedish Brown beans

2 tablespoons olive oil

1 medium onion, finely chopped

2 cloves garlic, minced

½ cup canned crushed tomatoes

2 tablespoons red wine vinegar

1 tablespoon dry red wine

2 tablespoons bourbon

3 tablespoons maple syrup or
unsulfured molasses

2 tablespoons prepared mustard

2 tablespoons prepared horseradish

2 teaspoons salt

2 teaspoons ground black pepper

Soak the beans overnight. Drain, put in a saucepan, cover with fresh water, and simmer until tender.

Preheat the oven to 325 degrees F. Oil a bean pot, casserole, or baking dish.

Sauté the onion in the oil until translucent, then add the garlic and cook for 1 minute more. Add the drained beans and all the other ingredients and stir occasionally over low heat for 10 or 15 minutes. Pour the mixture into the baking dish and cover with a lid or aluminum foil.

Bake for 1 hour 15 minutes. Check once or twice for drying; if the beans begin to look crusty or turn dark at the bottom, remove the dish from the oven and stir in a few tablespoons of water. Serve hot.

BLUE TEPARY BEAN SALAD

SERVES 8

*Small, colorfully speckled tepary beans look like tiny bird eggs. Their distinctive,
nutty flavor is best shown off in simple dishes in which they can shine.*

2 cups tepary beans

3 tablespoons olive oil

1 tablespoon tamari

Juice of 1 lemon

1 tablespoon wine vinegar

3 tablespoons chopped parsley

6 cherry tomatoes, cut into thin
wedges

Soak the beans overnight. Drain, cover with fresh water, and simmer until tender but not mushy.

Drain the cooked beans and put them in a bowl with the remaining ingredients, stirring well to distribute them. Let stand for at least 1 hour before serving. Refrigerate for longer periods, but allow the salad to come back to room temperature.

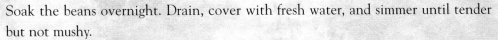

Yeasted Bean Fritters

SERVES 4

Beans are a heavyweight, as foods go, and this recipe uses yeast to leaven them. It is adapted from one in a useful pamphlet, "Cooking with Heirloom Beans," published by Fox Hollow Seed Co. of McGrann, Pennsylvania.

1¼ cups dry beans (4 cups cooked)
½ cup warm water
2 teaspoons sugar
1 tablespoon active dry yeast
1 medium chopped onion
5 tablespoons olive oil

1 cup flour
1 egg
2 tablespoons minced coriander
   leaves (optional)
1 teaspoon salt

Soak the beans overnight. Drain, and simmer them until tender. Place the warm water in a mixing bowl, stir in the sugar and yeast, and cover for 1 hour so that the yeast can froth.

Sauté the onion in 1 tablespoon olive oil. Put the drained beans, yeast mixture, and onion in a food processor or blender and puree. Stir in the flour, the beaten egg, optional coriander leaves, and salt. Allow this batter to sit 30 minutes to 1 hour for the yeast to work further. If you will not be cooking the fritters soon, refrigerate the batter for up to a day, and allow it to return to room temperature before continuing; the yeast will have generated a winelike fragrance you may prefer.

Use the remaining oil to fry the fritters, cooking them until golden brown. Serve hot with sour cream, yogurt, or maple syrup. Leftover fritters can be cut into small cubes and used as a meatlike addition to soups, adding them for the last 5 minutes of simmering.

RUNNER BEAN SOUP

Runner bean varieties are more than just vines with famously gorgeous blossoms.
The beans have a substantial, nutlike taste that makes them an excellent addition to soups.
They don't all taste alike, so use three or more for a fuller flavor. This recipe is
adapted from one developed by Phipps Country Store and Farm in Pescadero, California.
Valerie Phipps suggests serving the soup with hot cornbread.

2¼ cups shelly runner beans

1 onion, chopped

2 cloves garlic, minced

3 medium potatoes, cubed

3 carrots, cut into rounds

2 tablespoons olive oil

6 tablespoons balsamic vinegar

2 small zucchini, cut into rounds

6 tablespoons chopped parsley

3 tablespoons chopped cilantro

2 cups shredded chard, kale, or
  cabbage

3 teaspoons salt

Cook the beans until tender, and drain.

Sauté the onions, garlic, potatoes, and carrots in the oil until the onions are translucent and the vegetables are lightly browned, about 10 minutes. Scrape into a soup pot and add the beans, vinegar, and 7 cups water. Simmer for 10 minutes, or until the potatoes are nearly cooked. Add the remaining ingredients and simmer for 15 minutes more. Serve hot.

Snow Cap Chowder

SERVES 4

Snow Caps are so lovely that it seems a shame to sacrifice them to boiling water—
and the eventual digestion process. But this fishless, milk-based "chowder" is a worthy
cause. The beans retain their identity because they are cooked separately and
only then added to the other ingredients. The recipe comes from Potages U.S.A.

½ cup dry Snow Cap beans	3 tablespoons flour
3 medium potatoes, peeled and diced	½ teaspoon paprika
2 carrots, sliced	2 cups milk
4 tablespoons butter	2 cups stock
1 onion, chopped	Salt and pepper, to taste

After soaking the beans overnight, drain them, cover with fresh water, and simmer
until tender but not mushy (check them at 30 minutes). In the meanwhile, steam
the potatoes and carrots until just tender. Sauté the onions in the butter until soft,
and add the flour and paprika. Stir in the milk and stock until they just reach the
boiling point. Reduce the heat and add the steamed vegetables and the beans.
Season with salt and pepper and serve when all ingredients are hot.

Marinated Three-Bean Salad

SERVES 8

*Cathy Czapla says her Vermont family loves its heirloom beans, fresh
and dry, and puts both to use in a salad. For the fresh beans, they prefer Black
Valentine; for the dry, one of their top choices is Low's Champion. Substitute
whatever varieties you have on hand.*

1 cup fresh green or wax beans

1 cup dry beans, any combination
  of varieties, cooked

1 onion, minced

2 garlic cloves, minced

2 tablespoons olive oil

1 carrot, grated

3 tablespoons wine vinegar

Salt to taste

Cook the dried beans until tender, and the fresh beans until still just a little crisp. To
prevent the onion and garlic from shouting down the mild-flavored beans, sauté
them in the oil. Place all the ingredients in a bowl, mix well, and allow to sit for at
least 1 hour before serving. If you refrigerate the salad for longer periods, allow it to
reach room temperature before serving.

formanova

golden

Beets offer good eating on two levels—above ground and below. Most people are familiar only with the roots, and for good reason: The tired greens of supermarket beets are only fit for use as a handle. But the chardlike tops are excellent when fresh from your backyard or a farmers' market.

Beets are among the most intensely hued of plants, whether ornamental or edible, and take their name from the Celtic word for red. Gardeners have long been intrigued by beets of

BEETS

other colors, though. The roots also come in yellow and a dramatic candy-cane red and white. The greens, too, offer a modest show of their own, with ribs of red, gold, or pink-and-green stripes.

GROWING

Beets do best when grown before and after the dog days of midsummer. Plan on a spring planting and another late in summer.

Get a jump on the season by sowing in flats five or six weeks before you plan to set plants out in the garden. Or direct-seed once garden beds have been warmed by a touch of spring weather. To encourage germination, soak the seeds before planting for at least a couple of hours. Set them ¼ to ½ inch deep, 1 to 2 inches apart, in rows spaced 12 to 18 inches. Note that the corky-looking objects that slide out of the seed packet are in fact seedballs, each containing between two and a half-dozen seeds; that means you can look forward to thinning seedlings no matter how sparsely you sow. (Steam the seedlings for a sample of what is to come.) And if you've sown generously, thin again when the beets are young and tender; you can toss entire plants, greens and all, into a steamer basket. Don't be shy about thinning, because beets need hip room to develop properly—from 2 to 6 inches, depending on the width of the variety.

SAVING SEEDS

Saving beet seeds is a two-year project because this biennial doesn't flower and produce its seed clusters until the next growing season. (Or, this *usually* is a two-year affair; Pennsylvania Dutch farmers once believed that if a beet plant produced seeds the first year, as occasionally happens, there would be a death in the family.) Restrict yourself to growing a single variety each year if you will be saving seeds—beets have a talent for cross-pollinating over distances of a mile or more. Select good-looking beets from an August planting, trim the tops to an inch or so, and over-winter the roots in moist sand at between 35 and 50 degrees F. Plant the next spring. Tie up the stalks to stakes when they become tall and floppy, look for blossoms in June or July, and harvest the seeds in August. Cut off the tops and allow them to dry under cover, then strip off the seeds.

VARIETIES

Chioggia. No doubt this Italian heirloom owes its long life in part to its remarkable appearance. The root, when cut through, reveals sharply contrasting concentric circles of carmine and near white. Even the stems are dressed up with stripes of pinkish purple. To display the striking geometry of the roots, slice the raw beets into thin rounds and serve them with a dip or in a salad. But sample Chioggia first to check for bitterness. And here is a dilemma: The magnificent show is muted by cooking.

Formanova. This Danish variety is thought to date to the 1880s. It takes a bit more attention than other beets; the root extends above ground as it grows and should be covered with soil to prevent the skin from becoming roughened. The slim-hipped Formanova takes up relatively little space in the garden and is a good choice if your beds are pinched. The shape also recommends them for pickling, because you can fit a good number of whole beets in a pickling jar.

Formanova tastes sweet and free of bitterness even

when raw (another name for it is Cook's Delight); it is a good variety to grate as a colorful salad ingredient. The roots are uniform in diameter, which means they yield many same-size coins when sliced through. Harvest when young.

Golden. Plan on using more seeds for this variety, because germination is especially chancy. As soon as the seeds sprout, you know you're in for a vegetable of a different color: The little bits of unfolding life are brilliant yellow, distinguishing them from the nodding heads of other beet seedlings. The midribs of the leaves continue to glow like signals to remind you of the golden roots forming below.

Golden has been around since the early 1800s, but horticulturist Fearing Burr, Jr., noted in 1863 that yellow varieties were rarely grown because red was considered the proper color for a beet. Sampled straight out of the ground, Golden is reminiscent of raw potato, although not in an objectionable way. But if you note a lingering bitterness on the tongue, then bake, steam, or boil the beets to bring out their mild flavor. The greens, steamed or sautéed, are subtle as well.

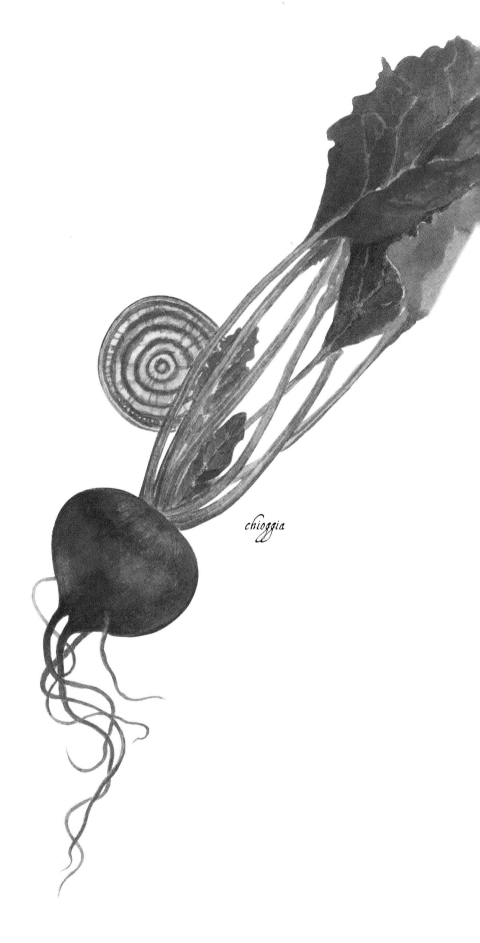

chioggia

Bi-Color Borscht

SERVES 6 TO 8

*In this recipe, a thick puree of beetroots and another of beet
tops are combined side by side in each soup bowl for a borscht with visual
interest. (If blended together, the tops and bottoms would
make an unfortunate color.) Use young beets if possible, with
roots measuring from 1 to 2 inches in diameter.*

RED BORSCHT

About 12 young beets with greens
2 red tomatoes, chopped
1 tablespoon red wine vinegar
2 tablespoons sweet vermouth
1 tablespoon olive oil
¼ teaspoon salt
½ teaspoon ground black pepper
1 cucumber, peeled and seeded
2 tablespoons chopped parsley
2 tablespoons chopped basil
1 tablespoon chopped cilantro
1 teaspoon ground cumin
Juice of 1 lemon
¼ teaspoon salt

GREEN BORSCHT

4 cups (packed) beet greens and
    other greens, such as chard
½ sweet onion, chopped
1 green bell pepper, cut into strips
3 cloves garlic, minced
1 tablespoon olive oil

Yogurt or sour cream, for serving
    (optional)

For the red borscht, cut the beet tops from the roots and set aside. Peel the roots if the skins are tough. Halve the smaller ones and quarter the larger ones to ensure even cooking. Steam the roots until tender, about 8 minutes. Transfer to a blender or food processor. Add the tomatoes, vinegar, vermouth, oil, salt, and pepper, and the cucumber, parsley, basil, cilantro, cumin, lemon juice, and salt. Puree until smooth. Pour into a bowl, cover, and refrigerate.

For the green borscht, rinse the reserved leaves well, discarding any that are yellowed or damaged, and supplement with other greens if necessary to make 4 cups. Sauté the onion, pepper strips, and garlic in oil. Transfer to the blender or food processor, and puree until smooth. Pour into a second bowl, and refrigerate.

The borscht is ready to assemble when chilled. Carefully spoon the red and green portions into each soup bowl, keeping a clear edge between the two. Use a flexible scraper to keep the halves separate as you pour. Straight edges are easiest, but you might also try a yin-yang pattern. Serve with a dollop of yogurt or sour cream in the center of each bowl, if you wish.

GOLDEN BEET SOUP WITH ORZO

SERVES 6 TO 8

The warm glow of golden beets suffuses this soup, and yellow bell peppers further punch up the color. Orzo adds substance, without dominating; this tiny pasta looks like plump melon seeds. The unsung ingredient is apple (preferably a somewhat tart variety, such as Granny Smith), which rounds out the other flavors.

8 cups stock, frozen or freshly made
¾ cup orzo
2 cups chopped sweet onion
2 tablespoons olive oil
5 to 6 cups peeled and julienned
   yellow beets

3 peeled and grated apples
1 cup finely shredded cabbage
2 teaspoons grated ginger
½ teaspoon ground black pepper
1 tablespoon tamari
1 yellow bell pepper, cut into strips

Defrost stock if you have some stashed away in the freezer, or prepare it your favorite way.

Cook the orzo in boiling salted water until slightly underdone, about 8 minutes (or 2 minutes less than specified on the package). Drain and set aside.

Using a soup pot over medium heat, sauté the onions in the oil until translucent, about 5 minutes. Add the beets, apples, cabbage, ginger, black pepper, and tamari, and continue to cook, stirring, for 3 minutes. Lower the heat, and add the stock.

Simmer, covered, for 45 minutes, stirring occasionally. Add the cooked orzo and bell pepper, and continue to cook for 10 minutes more. Serve hot.

🖉   *Beets are also used in Grilled Vegetable Lasagna (page 77) and Brilliant Julienned Kohlrabi (page 78).*

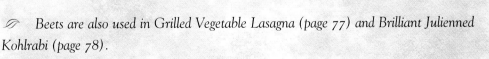

Cabbage is not the most glamorous of vegetables. It refuses to draw attention to itself, either in the garden or on a plate, and descriptions in seed catalogs and gardening books sound faintly apologetic ("classic," "a mainstay," and "a food supply you can depend on").

If cabbage doesn't inspire passion among gardeners in the way of tomatoes, hot peppers, and mesclun mixes, it may be because this crop

CABBAGE

stores so well; garden-grown heads don't have an immediately obvious advantage over those from the supermarket. And cabbage, as perhaps the most understated of vegetables, includes even fewer idiosyncratic varieties than, say, potatoes or turnips. Perhaps that's the main reason why the number of cabbage varieties available through mail-order seed catalogs has plummeted: Between 1981 and 1994, the number of green and red offerings fell from 136 to just

early jersey wakefield

lassø

75—and Thomas Jefferson grew at least 18 at Monticello. Another reason is that many gardeners choose to buy cabbage seedlings in flats rather than start their own from seed.

GROWING

Cabbages are classified as early, mid-season, late-season, and storage types. The early varieties are set out in spring; they work well for short growing seasons. Mid-season cabbages are sown after the last expected frost. Late-season cabbages are intended for fall harvest, and moderately cool temperatures allow you to keep them in the garden until needed; a chill in the air brings out the flavor of cabbages.

Direct sow seeds ½ inch deep, 5 seeds to the foot, in rows 2 to 3 feet apart; thin seedlings to every 18 to 24 inches, depending on the size of the variety. Indoors, set seeds ¼ inch deep and 2 inches apart in flats.

HARVESTING

Cabbages are ready to roll when firm and fully formed. Early varieties are quick to mature, and should be harvested promptly before they can crack open. They can be stored for just a month or two, given near-freezing temperatures and high humidity. Late varieties can be allowed to stay out in the garden; a light frost or two will sweeten their flavor, but they should be brought in for storage in a cool place before hard frosts. Rather than yanking the plants, roots and all, try cutting the heads so that as much of the stem as possible is left intact; you may see small heads forming

for a second, especially tender harvest. Here's a time-honored trick for slowing the development of mature heads you don't want to harvest right away: Grasp the head and twist a quarter of the way around, so that some roots are severed. Younger heads store best.

SAVING SEEDS

You face a two-year project, and also the chance that your prize cabbage variety will swap pollen with both other cabbages and cabbage family relatives. Keep plants intended for seed at least 300 feet from them.

Use a loose mulch to help plants overwinter, or in colder zones, unearth the plants, roots and all, and keep them indoors in a cool, humid spot for setting out in spring. In the second year, you can help the flower stalk to come forth by slashing an **X** in the top of each cabbage's head. Wait until the seed heads turn brown before collecting the seeds.

VARIETIES

Early Jersey Wakefield. Few heirloom vegetable varieties have remained as dominant as Early Jersey Wakefield. The conical heads mature early and weigh in at 2 to 3 pounds. Young leaves can be used as a salad adjunct.

Lassø. This early-heading Danish red cabbage takes its name from an island in Denmark's archipelago. The heads aren't large, but they form a firm, trim ball with few outer leaves.

DANISH SWEET-SOUR RED CABBAGE

SERVES 6 TO 8

This recipe waves the Danish flag because it was passed down through the author's Danish-American family. But sweet-sour red cabbage is a dish that also has circulated freely through northern Germany and the North Sea culture without boundaries known as Frisia. The aromas of the spicy cabbage are as festive as those of baking pies, and this is a good dish for Thanksgiving, when cabbages, apples, and cider are all plentiful. The caraway-flavored aquavit liquor and the butter are optional but very Danish, not to be omitted lightly. This dish tastes best if made a day ahead and reheated before serving. Prepare the recipe in a very large skillet or divide ingredients between 2 smaller skillets.

2 onions, chopped

3 tablespoons olive oil

4 cloves garlic, minced

1 head red cabbage, chopped

4 sweet-tart apples, peeled, cored, and chopped

2 tablespoons red wine vinegar

2 tablespoons maple syrup or brown sugar

1 cup cider without preservatives or orange juice

1 cup malty beer

3 tablespoons bourbon

2 tablespoons freshly grated ginger

1 tablespoon ground coriander

2 teaspoons ground cinnamon

1 teaspoon ground cardamom

1 teaspoon grated nutmeg

1 teaspoon caraway seeds (omit if using aquavit)

2 teaspoons hot pepper sauce

2 teaspoons salt

2 teaspoons ground black pepper

3 tablespoons aquavit (optional)

3 tablespoons butter (optional)

Juice of 1 lemon

Sauté the onions in the oil until translucent, about 5 minutes, then the garlic. Add the cabbage and apples and stir-fry for 1 or 2 minutes as best you can; the cabbage will become more manageable as it cooks down. Add all the remaining ingredients except the butter and lemon juice, mix well, and cover. Simmer for 1 hour, stirring occasionally to distribute the flavors evenly. Add more cider as necessary to prevent sticking. With 5 minutes to go, add the butter, if you wish, and the lemon juice. Stir well, cover, and simmer until the hour is up. Serve hot or let stand overnight, refrigerated, and reheat.

SIMMERED CABBAGE WEDGES

In this variation on an old French recipe, cabbage—either green or red—is joined by acidic apples and fingerling potatoes (small varieties that don't need to be cut for this recipe). If Granny Smith apples aren't available, use Northern Spies, Winesaps, old cider types, or not-quite-ripe apples of any variety. All are simmered in sizable chunks, so that there is a farmhouse quality about the dish. Cutting a head of cabbage according to the number of family members is a traditional American practice as well. Serve this stew alone with crusty bread or as a side dish.

2 medium onions, coarsely chopped

2 tablespoons olive oil

4 tablespoons wine vinegar

½ cup dry vermouth

1 teaspoon salt

1 large head green or red cabbage, cut into 6 or 8 wedges, cored

4 to 5 cups fingerling potatoes

4 Granny Smith apples, peeled, cut into 8 wedges, cored

4 tablespoons butter

Choose a skillet with a tight-fitting lid, making sure it is large enough to hold the ingredients; a soup pot will also work. Sauté the onions in the oil until soft, about 5 minutes. Reduce the heat and add the vinegar, vermouth, ¾ cup water, and salt. Place the cabbage wedges and the potatoes in the skillet and simmer, covered, for 45 minutes. Add the apples and continue to simmer for 45 minutes more, or until the largest of the potatoes are tender when poked with a fork. Serve hot in soup bowls with some of the broth. Top each portion with about ½ tablespoon butter.

oxheart

As with other root crops, carrots are omitted from the spring plans of many gardeners because of an untested assumption that freshness isn't an issue with something grown in the ground. In fact, your own carrots will have an herbaceous zing

CARROTS

missing from those in the supermarket. And you may find that this quality is all it takes to promote carrots from an obligation to a pleasure.

The carrot is one of those good-for-you vegetables that many people consume the way they do vitamin pills—dutifully. Even when they are prepared simply, the differences between heirloom carrots are subtle. In the words of Maryland gardener Sharon Koury, "Carrots just don't move me; they're just kind of *orange*, aren't they?" But there is obvious interest among heirloom gardeners in international varieties, trafficking seed from the Netherlands, United Kingdom, Poland, France, Germany, Algeria, India, Afganistan, and Japan.

GROWING

Do a good job of loosening the soil down to a depth of at least a foot and evict rocks of any size while you're at it. Gardening books direct you to lavish compost on every living thing, but carrots especially will benefit

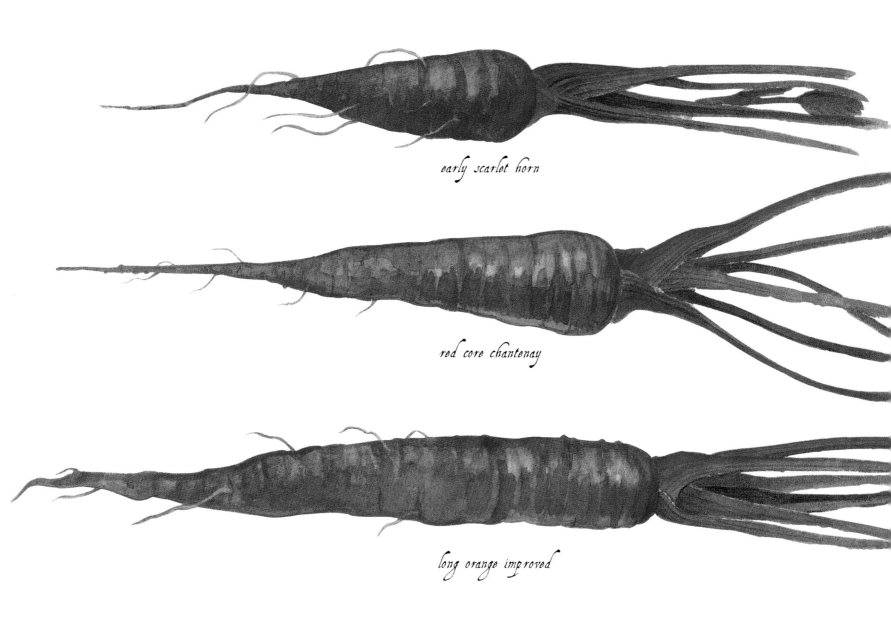

early scarlet horn

red core chantenay

long orange improved

from its soil-leavening effect. Don't use manure later than the fall before planting seed—the carrots will respond to fresher stuff by enthusiastically growing huge tops. If you're a real carrot fan, plan on seeding every two or three weeks from early spring through midsummer for a continuous harvest. Set seeds ¼ inch deep, 3 seeds to the inch and spaced in rows 12 inches apart. Cover the seeds with fine soil. Thin plants to 3 inches within rows. Once carrots are several inches high, they'll benefit from a moisture-conserving mulch.

If the soil is loamy and loose in your flower beds, try interplanting carrots for the ornament of their lacy tops.

HARVESTING

Baby carrots should be ready to harvest in 45 to 55 days. Later than that, be guided by size—carrots are at their most tender and flavorful when no more than 1 inch in diameter.

SAVING SEEDS

Carrots will cross with each other and with their country cousin, Queen Anne's lace. To save seeds from a variety, it should be isolated at least 200 feet from either potential pollen source—a thousand feet would be better. Harvest roots before the first hard frost can get to them and store in sand in a cool basement. Set them in the garden the next spring and pick the ripened seed heads.

VARIETIES

Early Scarlet Horn. Not "horn" for a peculiar shape, but for Hoorn, a town out on the string of Frisian Islands off the Dutch coast. The short roots are juicy, mild, and particularly delicious; it's understandable that this variety has been in cultivation for some four hundred years. Try harvesting as baby carrots for optimal flavor and texture.

Long Orange Improved. This yellow-green cored carrot is mild, with a slight taste of soap and a perfumey scent. It dates back to the mid-1800s.

Oxheart. This high-yielding, long-keeping French carrot is good for freezing and canning. With its blunt shape, it grows better than most in heavy soils.

Red Core Chantenay. This is one of several varieties descended from Chantenays brought over from Europe in the 1800s. The flavor improves with storage; fresh out of the garden, they taste herby and slightly wild, and may have a hint of soapy flavor characteristic of certain heirloom carrots. In a taste test of fifteen varieties at Seeds of Change, this Chantenay rated highest.

MASHED CARROTS AND TURNIPS

A traditional farmhouse way to make use of a bumper crop of carrots is to steam and mash them along with other root vegetables, just as you would potatoes. Heirloom gardener Donna Irwin recalls that her Massachusetts grandmother often mashed carrots along with turnips.

Begin with roughly equal amounts of carrots and turnips, cubed or chopped any which way to speed cooking. Steam until tender, then mash along with butter, wine vinegar, salt, and ground black pepper, either manually or with a food processor.

GRATED CARROT SALAD

For a quick salad, reduce a pound of carrots with a grater.
Include a touch of raw beet for the color, if you wish.

1 pound carrots, grated
¼ small red beet, grated (optional)
1 tablespoon olive oil
1 tablespoon red wine vinegar

1 teaspoon freshly grated ginger
8 to 12 black olives, pitted and
   slivered

Grate the carrots and beet, if you'll be using it, and toss in a serving bowl to combine. Combine the oil, vinegar, ginger, and olives in a small bowl and mix well. Stir this mixture into the grated vegetables. Let stand for at least 30 minutes before serving.

Carrots are also used in the recipe for Brilliant Julienned Kohlrabi (page 78).

48 · A CELEBRATION OF HEIRLOOM VEGETABLES

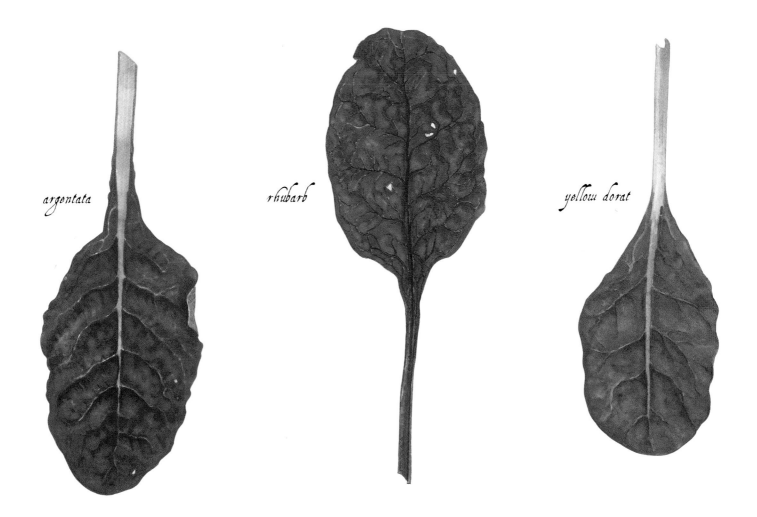

argentata *rhubarb* *yellow dorat*

CHARD

Chard is a mild-mannered green that deserves more respect. That was as true a century ago as today; in his *Handbook of Plants*, published in 1890, Peter Henderson dismissed chard as a stand-in for spinach that found favor with the "laboring class."

Chard is a close relative of the beet, and in common with that crop, all varieties are visually attractive. A white or brilliant-hued midrib contrasts dramatically with the deep green leaves. This is the living legacy of growers having selected handsome plants over the centuries. Clearly, a preference for high-colored varieties isn't just a new, boutique gardening trend but a natural response on the part of those of us who till the soil.

Chard can be steamed, sautéed, stir-fried, and added to soups and pasta dishes. Use it to moderate the sharp flavor of chicory and dandelion greens. And try offering it to children for whom spinach has too much flavor (and often too much gritty soil trapped in the crinkly leaves).

GROWING

Ordinary, well-drained garden soil will suit chard. Consider planting chard among robust flowers and bushes as an interesting, spirited annual.

For an early crop, start seeds in flats. Or begin sowing directly in the garden about two weeks before your last frost date. Seeds should be planted ½ inch deep, spaced every 2 inches in rows 18 to 24 inches apart. Thin young plants to 8 to 10 inches apart. With care, you can use some of these thinnings to fill in any gaps in the rows; the rest can be added raw to salads. Sow through to late summer for successive crops.

HARVESTING

Begin harvesting when the outer leaves reach 6 to 10 inches in length. Newer growth will take their place.

Chard can handle frosts, allowing you to continue picking right through the winter in milder zones.

SAVING SEEDS

Allow some plants to grow out and produce seed—a process that runs into the next season because chard is a biennial and doesn't blossom and set seed until the second year. In cooler zones, mulch the plants to help them through the winter. The plants will flower the following year. Pick the browning seedpods and allow them to dry completely under cover. These seeds aren't likely to closely mimic their parents, because chard pollen may ride the winds for a mile or so.

For a greater range of plants to choose from, you can sow the Breeder's Rainbow chard mix offered by Peters Seed and Research. These seeds are in a state of genetic flux and look as though they can't quite make up their minds; for example, the midrib of one plant may be a curious in-between salmony shade. The gardener intervenes by studying the row of mismatched—but unfailingly attractive—plants and choosing one or more on the basis of production, adaptability, taste, color, or whatever.

VARIETIES

Argentata. The name refers to the silvery effect of the white midrib. This old Italian variety isn't especially attractive, but its exceptional flavor—mild and refreshing, with a hint of tartness—makes up for a lack of visual splash.

rainbow

Rhubarb. Also known as Ruby, this is an old standard, having been cultivated since before the Civil War and still available in supermarket produce departments. The flavor is somewhat earthy and similar to spinach. Rhubarb makes such a display in the garden that you may feel reluctant to harvest it. Interplant with Argentata for a still more impressive show.

Rainbow. Rainbow chard, or Five-Color Silverbeet, is a collection of five variously colored strains that went out of commercial distribution in the 1980s and was later rescued by Seed Savers Exchange. It has been their best-selling item and is something of a symbol of the worthwhile vegetables that may be lost through the indifference of large-scale seed companies. Two of the five colors—white, pink, red, orange, and yellow—are shown here. Interplant this variety with Purple Vienna kohlrabi for a display that would make blossoms redundant.

Yellow Dorat. The tender, light yellow-green leaves are attractive in their own quiet way. You can strip the wide stalks from the leaves and cook them as you would asparagus—an intriguing traditional cooking method. Dorat is a Danish improvement on an older favorite, Lucullus.

CHARD FRITTATA

SERVES 4

*Chard seems to lend itself to eggy recipes. With little effort, you can rinse a few
leaves, tear them in strips, and stir them into a couple of eggs for a quick omelet.
A frittata is more ambitious—and impressive enough to serve to guests.*

*This recipe requires a bit of juggling; you'll have to flip the partially cooked
frittata out of the pan and return it to cook the other side. If this daunts you (or if
you plan to increase the quantities for more servings), you can make the
flipping go easier by cooking two smaller frittatas.*

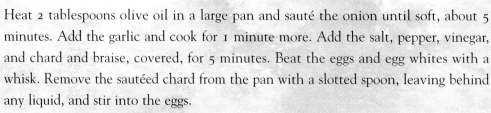

Olive oil	2 tablespoons wine vinegar
1 small onion, minced	6 cups coarsely chopped chard
2 cloves garlic, minced	2 large eggs
¼ teaspoon salt	8 large egg whites
Ground black pepper, to taste	2 tablespoons grated romano cheese

Heat 2 tablespoons olive oil in a large pan and sauté the onion until soft, about 5 minutes. Add the garlic and cook for 1 minute more. Add the salt, pepper, vinegar, and chard and braise, covered, for 5 minutes. Beat the eggs and egg whites with a whisk. Remove the sautéed chard from the pan with a slotted spoon, leaving behind any liquid, and stir into the eggs.

Dry the pan, return it to low heat, and spread a bit of olive oil in it with a broad plastic spatula. Pour the egg-and-chard mixture into the pan and cook without stirring, covering to encourage the eggs to set. As soon as the eggs appear firm, about 10 minutes, slide the spatula under the frittata for a moment to make sure it is free from the pan. Holding a baking sheet firmly over the pan, invert the whole works. Lift the pan, and you should be looking at the nicely browned bottom of the frittata.

Return the pan to the heat and slide the upended frittata into it. Sprinkle the grated cheese over the top, put on the lid, and cook for about 3 minutes. Divide the frittata into wedges and serve immediately.

CHARD CALZONES

A novel way to steam chard is in the dough pockets of calzones. Serve them with a tureen of warm tomato sauce if you like. There is no need to precook the greens. You also can use broccoli rabe or young mustard and turnip greens.

DOUGH

- 1⅓ cups warm water
- 1 tablespoon active dry yeast
- 1 teaspoon sugar
- 1 tablespoon olive oil
- 1 teaspoon salt
- 2 cups unbleached all-purpose flour

FILLING

- 3 cups finely chopped chard
- 1½ cups finely chopped sweet onions
- 3 cloves garlic, minced
- 1 cup grated provolone cheese
- 2 tablespoons olive oil
- 2 tablespoons balsamic vinegar
- ½ teaspoon salt
- Cornmeal for dusting

Pour the warm water into a large mixing bowl and stir the yeast and sugar into it. Cover and set aside for 10 minutes.

Stir in the oil, salt, and flour, using a sturdy spoon and strong strokes to avoid forming lumps. Turn the dough out onto a flour-dusted countertop or breadboard and knead for 10 minutes. Add more flour as necessary to keep the dough from sticking to your hands and the kneading surface. Return the dough to the mixing bowl, cover with a lid or wax paper, and set aside to rise until doubled in bulk, about 2 hours.

Combine the chard, onions, garlic, and cheese in a bowl. Stir in the oil, vinegar, and salt. Set aside.

When the dough has risen, preheat the oven to 400 degrees F. Dust a baking sheet with cornmeal. Divide the dough into 5 equal pieces. Shape the pieces into balls and allow them to rest for 5 minutes. Using the oiled palms of your hands, gently press each piece into an oval shape roughly 10 by 14 inches. The dough should not be so thin that it will tear when handled. Distribute a fifth of the filling on half of an oval, keeping the edges clear to allow sealing the calzone. Fold the empty half of the oval over the filled half and pinch around the edges. Place the calzones on the baking sheet.

Bake for 25 minutes, or until golden on the bottom. Serve hot.

dentarella

biondissima

red treviso

castelfranco

puntarella

spadona

Chicory's unfamiliarity to Americans has to do not only with its chameleon nature—as a wildflower, vegetable, and coffee adulterant—but also with its sharp taste, suggested by the toothed leaves. It is only now winning a place in garden plots, following its appearance in the mescluns and other salads of trend-conscious restaurants.

CHICORY

The bitterness of the plant isn't tamed by cooking, but the relative sweetness of virgin olive or almond oil seems to moderate chicory's assertiveness when sautéed. On the other hand, the greens bring out the sweetness in butter.

Even the names of chicories are foreign—they sound like the names of Cinderella's stepsisters, and all do have strong personalities to match. Several chicories honor the northern Italian towns where they were developed.

GROWING

Chicory is favored by cool weather. Seed cutting varieties directly in the garden as soon as the soil can be worked. Seed again eight weeks before the fall's first frost for a second crop. Sow ¼ inch deep, thinning to 6 inches between plants.

Heading chicories need a later start, from the end of spring through early July. They are allowed to grow through the summer, showing just a hint of the red and burgundy hues to come, and then cut back to the ground around the first of September. This seems a violent, destructive act, but the plant's vegetative flywheel is spinning, and the roots will push out small, compact heads for an October or November harvest. Leave just an inch or so of stem from which new heads can sprout.

HARVESTING

Chicory grows enthusiastically and will leap into tall, orderly stands. The taller, the more bitter, so start snipping with scissors when leaves are just 6 inches or so for salads and sautéeing. Try mixing chicory with milder greens that will benefit from a rabble-rouser in their midst. Allow at least a few plants to continue growing for the cool-blue flowers they'll produce in the heat of midsummer.

SAVING SEEDS

Collect the browned seed heads before birds and the weather disperse their contents.

VARIETIES

Biondissima. This relatively light-colored chicory is used in mesclun mixes, and also can be harvested at a larger size for salads and sautéing.

Castelfranco. This variety can be snipped as the leaves come up, or you can allow it to develop rounded heads on its own, without cutting back as for other heading chicories. Castelfranco cooks to a relatively soft consistency and has the taste of a bitter spinach.

Dentarella. Dentarella is easier to get to know than others. It is pleasantly mild and cooks up into greens that taste like cardoon, a leafy artichoke relative not often seen in North America.

Puntarella. The skinny, toothed leaves somehow look bitter, and in fact this variety can have a sharp, almost metallic taste. It will overwinter in most zones.

Red Treviso. A heading variety, more bitter than some, with a slight flavor of artichoke. Its wine-red coloration develops after summer's green phase. Cut back to form small heads.

Spadona. Spadona is relatively mild, with a good toothsome crunch. The flavor hints at spinach.

Sautéed Chicory and Pasta

Serves 4

This recipe uses chicory in much the way that pesto harnesses the big-bore flavor of basil. Almond oil has a perfumed sweetness that is especially complementary to chicory's bluntness, but a fruity olive oil will do as well.

3 tablespoons almond or olive oil

4 cloves garlic, minced

2 heaping tablespoons pine nuts

6 black olives, such as kalamata, pitted and slivered

4 heaping tablespoons chopped dried tomatoes

2 tablespoons balsamic or red wine vinegar

3 to 4 cups chopped chicory

3 heaping tablespoons grated asiago cheese

Hot pasta

Put water on to boil for the pasta. Heat the oil in a skillet and sauté the garlic. Add the pine nuts and toast briefly. Add the olives, dried tomatoes, vinegar, and chicory. Continue to sauté for 6 to 8 minutes, covered, stirring occasionally.

Meanwhile, cook the pasta until al dente.

Drain the pasta, add it to the skillet, and stir to mix well. Divide among 4 plates and top each with cheese. Serve immediately.

kailan

Although Asian greens may not seem like a part of homespun Americana, they tend to be long-standing varieties and have been met with interest by North American gardeners. Three of these brassicas are shown here and on the next page. They are called by several names in several languages and dialects—Japanese, Cantonese, Mandarin, and English—and there isn't even agreement on their Latin species names.

Ching-Chiang is a form of bok choy, variously known as pak choi, Chinese celery cabbage, mustard cabbage, white-stemmed cabbage, and Chinese mustard. Choy Sum, also known as Cai

CHINESE GREENS

Xin and white flowering cabbage, is a flowering, nonheading cabbage. Kailan goes by Gai Lohn, Gai Choi, Kaai Laan Tsoi, white flowering broccoli, Chinese broccoli, and Chinese kale.

GROWING

For the earliest start in spring, sow seeds indoors in cells or small pots one month before your last frost date; they should be ¼ inch deep. In the garden, space transplants 6 to 12 inches apart, depending on variety. If you sow in midsummer for a fall crop, you'll have a better chance of getting a good yield of leaves before plants invest their energy in flowering.

HARVESTING

Ching-Chiang can be used for just the tender leaves, if you wish; or, when a flowering shoot appears, snip that as well and toss it into a stir-fry. Or take entire plants; they are small enough in the dwarf form to be stir-fried or steamed whole. Expect to begin harvesting within 30 days.

Choy Sum offers a double harvest: You start by cutting the broad-ribbed leaves, and later the flowering shoots. Leave some shoots behind to allow the plants to keep on producing.

All parts of Kailan are edible. Begin by harvesting the main flowering shoot, then the side shoots as they grow. Or harvest the entire plant just six weeks after sowing, without waiting for the shoot.

SAVING SEEDS

Let the seedpods dry on the plant until brittle, then bring them inside and shake the seeds free.

dwarf ching-chiang

choy sum

VARIETIES

Dwarf Ching-Chiang. You may have seen this attractive, compact looseleaf cabbage at Asian grocers. The dwarf form, illustrated here, has short, stocky petioles and looks something like the heads of broccoli rabe. It has a mild flavor and a texture that is suited for stir-frying. The yellow, faintly fragrant flower clusters can be cooked as well.

Choy Sum. This mainland China variety is valued for the young, tender leaves and flower stalks. It excels in stir-fries. The dwarf version, harvested at just 3 to 8 inches tall, is shown here.

Kailan. Kailan is especially attractive, with its white flowers and cool-green leaves, so consider a location where it won't be obscured by other crops. It is milder in flavor and less chewy than Western kale—and Western broccoli, for that matter.

CATCHALL STIR-FRY

SERVES 4

A wok works by melding together ingredients at high temperature, with an assist from tamari (soy sauce) and a sour constituent, such as vinegar or lemon juice. Many vegetables take to this quick, intense treatment as if the wok were their planned destiny.

With little effort you can make a stir-fry leap international borders, using ingredients emblematic of Thai, Indian, Mexican, Italian, or Moroccan cuisine. Before you lay on the pecorino and oregano, however, keep in mind that a well-seasoned steel wok has a memory, bringing a suggestion of past meals to the ingredients of the day. The cross-pollination of oregano and bok choy may set off a dissonance of the palate that you'll find disturbing—or intriguing, pointing the way to new recipes.

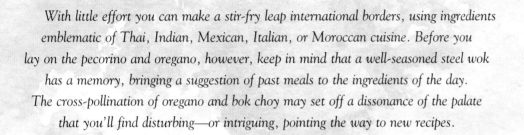

1 tablespoon olive oil

1 tablespoon sesame oil

1 pound tofu, cubed

2 ripe bell peppers, cut into strips

3 cloves garlic, thinly sliced

2 tablespoons tamari

2 tablespoons wine vinegar
   or rice vinegar

1 tablespoon freshly grated ginger

6 cups coarsely chopped greens

Juice of 1 lemon

3 tablespoons sesame seeds, toasted

Hot cooked rice or pasta, for serving

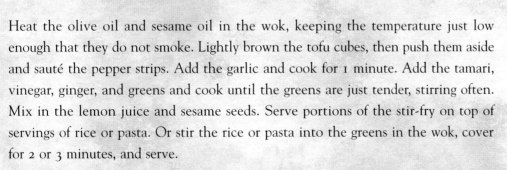

Heat the olive oil and sesame oil in the wok, keeping the temperature just low enough that they do not smoke. Lightly brown the tofu cubes, then push them aside and sauté the pepper strips. Add the garlic and cook for 1 minute. Add the tamari, vinegar, ginger, and greens and cook until the greens are just tender, stirring often. Mix in the lemon juice and sesame seeds. Serve portions of the stir-fry on top of servings of rice or pasta. Or stir the rice or pasta into the greens in the wok, cover for 2 or 3 minutes, and serve.

Eggplant, like okra, is something of a problem child—attractive enough but not the easiest of vegetables to prepare in the kitchen. This challenge is compounded by using oversize, less-than-fresh specimens from the supermarket. The showroom-glossy finish of the familiar black eggplant can hide flesh that has gone punky, seedy, and insipid.

As a gardener, you can have young, fresh eggplants just outside the kitchen door. They won't be bitter, so you don't have to go through the messy ritual of salting them. Smaller fruits don't even have to be peeled. On top of that, you have a choice of varieties with distinctive shapes, colors, and flavors. Turkish Orange and Listada de Gandia are so vividly colored that they won't look out of place in a mixed border, displaying yellow-centered lavender flowers and brilliant fruits. The plants are manageable in size. Just keep the flea beetles from making skeletons of the attractive foliage.

EGGPLANT

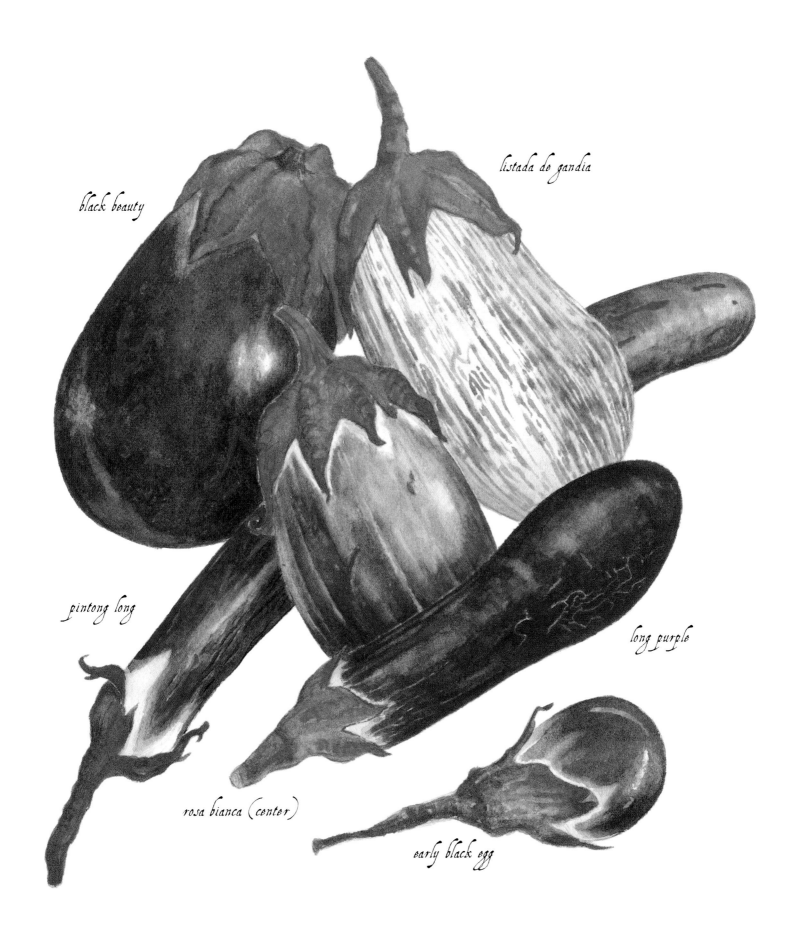

black beauty

listada de gandia

pintong long

long purple

rosa bianca (center)

early black egg

GROWING

Sow seeds indoors ¼ inch deep, 8 weeks before setting out plants. Provide bottom heat of 80 to 90 degrees F. Seedlings do best around 70 degrees. A week of 60-degree temperatures just before moving to the garden will prepare them for transplanting.

Eggplants are ready to be set out when the weather has moderated and daytime temperatures reach the 60s. Place transplants 18 inches apart, in rows spaced every 2 to 3 feet. To prevent diseases, do not grow eggplants in soil that has recently hosted them or other members of the nightshade family. Flea beetles are not so easily circumvented. If they threaten to skeletonize the foliage, treat with rotenone or pyrethrum, or keep them at bay with floating row covers.

HARVESTING

Harvest the fruits before they get to their full size. Overripe eggplant tastes bitter, and prompt picking encourages production. Be sure to cut fruits from the plant rather than trying to twist or tear them free. Use them right after harvest to enjoy them at their best. Do not store them in the refrigerator.

SAVING SEEDS

Take seeds from eggplants that are past ripe and have lost their glossiness. Spoon out the seedy center and rinse in a sieve to separate the seeds. Dry them on paper towels.

PURPLE

Black Beauty. This is the best known of eggplants in North America, having become something of the standard variety since their introduction in 1902. Although less than promising when mature and seedy, the smaller fruits are mild and flavorful.

Early Black Egg. The fruits of this Japanese variety will reach 7 inches in length but are at their tenderest when picked smaller. This variety performs well in cooler areas with short growing seasons.

Listada de Gandia. Listada is handsome in the garden and a mild-mannered delight in the kitchen. You can encourage the fruits to grow straight by staking plants as you would tomatoes.

Long Purple. This Italian eggplant is highly prolific, producing at least four fruits per plant if conditions favor it.

Pintong Long. Named for a town on Taiwan, this eggplant cooks down to a tender consistency, with a notably sweet flavor. If you're tired of rubbery, bitter eggplant, give Pintong a try. You may be able to preview it by buying a sample at an Asian market.

Rosa Bianca. This beautifully colored Italian variety has tender, mild-flavored flesh that makes you wonder why cooks put up with salting the bitterness out of huge, deep-purple eggplants.

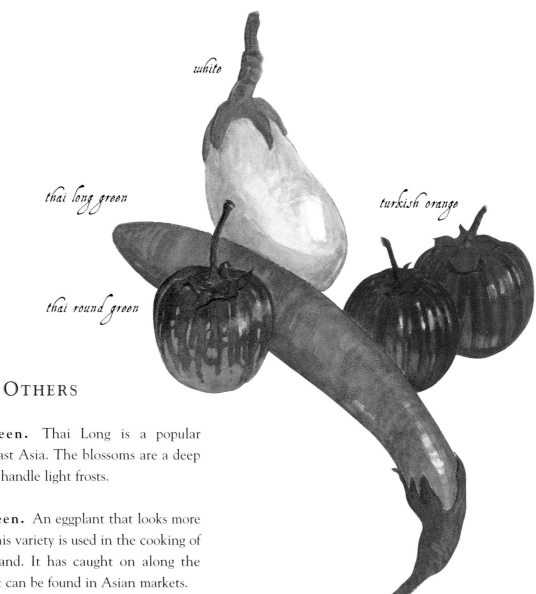

white

thai long green

turkish orange

thai round green

OTHERS

Thai Long Green. Thai Long is a popular heirloom in Southeast Asia. The blossoms are a deep lavender. Plants can handle light frosts.

Thai Round Green. An eggplant that looks more like a green apple, this variety is used in the cooking of Vietnam and Thailand. It has caught on along the West Coast, where it can be found in Asian markets.

Turkish Orange. Few visitors to your garden will fail to remark on this eggplant, if you let it ripen to the reddish orange shown here. However, you're also apt to hear remarks if you serve it to them in this advanced state of ripeness—Turkish Orange is fragrant and sweet when picked green, and bitter when flaming orange. Use it for an accent in such dishes as ratatouille and tomato-based pasta sauces.

White. White eggplants tend to taste milder than purple varieties of the same shape. Although Thomas Jefferson grew white eggplants at Monticello, they were regarded more as decorative curiosities through the 1800s and "less esteemed," according to Fearing Burr in his 1863 book, *The Field and Garden Vegetables of America.*

BABY IMAM BAYILDI

SERVES 4

*If the various vegetables are arranged in the baking dish with care, this
eastern Mediterranean recipe is attractive enough to be brought to the table for serving.*

6 or so baby eggplants (to total
  about 2 pounds)

3 red potatoes, diced

1 zucchini

2 onions

6 tablespoons olive oil

4 garlic cloves, minced

3 to 6 tomatoes, finely chopped (or
  2 cups canned crushed tomatoes)

12 to 18 kalamata olives,
  pitted and slivered

1 tablespoon sweet vermouth

Juice of 1 lemon

½ teaspoon rosemary, chopped

½ teaspoon oregano, chopped

½ teaspoon ground cinnamon

¼ cup parsley, chopped

½ cup crumbled feta cheese

Preheat the oven to bake at 425 degrees F. Cut the tops off the eggplants, slit them
deeply from top to bottom, and pry apart with the fingers. Cut the potatoes into
¾-inch cubes. Cut the zucchini across the middle, and quarter both halves
lengthwise. Cut the onions in eighths, slicing down through their tops.

Spread 2 tablespoons of olive oil around the inside of a baking dish. As you
arrange the cut vegetables in the dish, drizzle another 2 tablespoons of olive oil and
roll the pieces about so that they are coated on all sides. Arrange the vegetables in a
pleasing way, both for the sake of appearance and so that portions will have a mix of
each vegetable.

Bake the vegetables for 30 minutes. Begin preparing the sauce by heating the
remaining 2 tablespoons of olive oil in a pan and sautéing the minced garlic. Add
the tomatoes (using sauce tomatoes if you have them), olives, vermouth, lemon
juice, and spices. Simmer for 5 minutes if using canned sauce; if you're using fresh
tomatoes, simmer with the lid off until no longer watery. Chop the parsley and stir it
into the tomato mixture after taking it off the heat.

Remove the vegetables from the oven. Spoon the tomato mixture around the
vegetables, allowing them to show through; place some of the mixture inside each of
the eggplants as well. Sprinkle the cheese over the top. Bake for another 15 minutes.
Serve with yogurt and pita bread.

EGGPLANT DINNER PANCAKES

*And what did Americans make from eggplant before eggplant parm? Pancakes.
This recipe is adapted from one that appeared in The Garden Magazine
in 1908. The recipe can easily be modified for breakfast. Add ¼ cup peeled and
grated apple to the eggplant puree before measuring to determine how
much flour to use. Add ½ teaspoon ground cinnamon to the flour, omit the
black pepper and parsley, and halve the amount of salt.*

2 to 3 medium Black Beauty
   eggplants, or equivalent
   (about 4 pounds)

2 tablespoons red wine vinegar

4 egg whites, whisked

3 tablespoons chopped parsley

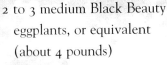

¼ cup unbleached all-purpose flour
   for each cup of pureed eggplant

1½ teaspoons baking powder

2 teaspoons salt

1 teaspoon ground black pepper

Oil, for frying

Peel the eggplants and cut them into 1-inch cubes. Fill a medium saucepan with water and add the vinegar. Add the eggplant and bring to a boil. Reduce the heat and simmer until tender, about 10 minutes. (You may have to hold down the floating cubes with a vegetable steaming basket so that they cook properly.) Remove the softened eggplant with a slotted spoon and reduce it to a smooth pulp in a food processor. Measure the pulp to determine how much flour will be added. Add the whisked egg whites and the parsley to the puree.

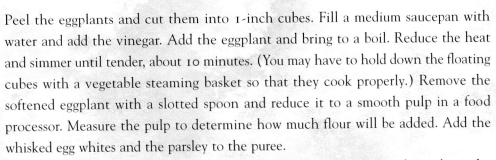

In another bowl, combine ¼ cup flour for each cup of pureed eggplant, the baking powder, salt, and black pepper. Stir these dry ingredients into the puree. Heat a lightly oiled nonstick skillet and cook the batter as you would standard pancakes, browning on both sides. Serve hot.

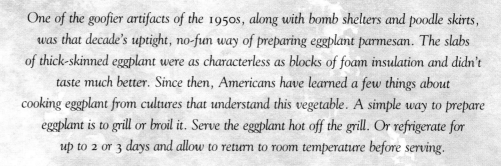

GRILLED EGGPLANT

One of the goofier artifacts of the 1950s, along with bomb shelters and poodle skirts, was that decade's uptight, no-fun way of preparing eggplant parmesan. The slabs of thick-skinned eggplant were as characterless as blocks of foam insulation and didn't taste much better. Since then, Americans have learned a few things about cooking eggplant from cultures that understand this vegetable. A simple way to prepare eggplant is to grill or broil it. Serve the eggplant hot off the grill. Or refrigerate for up to 2 or 3 days and allow to return to room temperature before serving.

Italian or Asian eggplants
Olive oil
Balsamic vinegar

Tamari or salt
Garlic cloves, minced
Parsley, chopped

Cut the stem ends off the eggplants, and slice them lengthwise into slabs between ¼ and ½ inch thick. Prepare the marinade from the oil, vinegar, tamari or salt, and garlic, using your judgment as to quantities.

Place the slices in it at least an hour before broiling, if possible. Grill on one side, then turn them and brush marinade on the grilled surface, keeping an eye on the slices to prevent them from drying out. Garnish with the parsley.

It is said that kale was introduced to North America by Benjamin Franklin, returning from a visit to Scotland. Two centuries later, most people know kale only as a garnish with as much gustatory appeal as the dusty little trees on model train layouts. And yet the varieties shown here are tender, sweet—and vitamin intensive, although the taste doesn't shout the fact.

wild red

Kale is easy to grow, too. It will cruise right through fall, giving you a good reason to keep visiting the garden even when the beds are covered with snow. There isn't a great deal of trade in

KALE

kale seeds among heirloom gardeners, but one company, Peters Seed and Research, offers unstable strains so that the backyard plant breeder can identify the best of many variations, save seeds the following season, and gradually customize a variety.

verdura

GROWING

Allow kale to sidestep the hottest summer weather by planting a fall crop three months before the first anticipated frost. You can also squeeze in an early summer crop by sowing seed indoors and transplanting when weather permits. In the garden, sow seeds ¼ to ½ inch deep and 1 inch apart, in rows spaced 18 to 30 inches. Thin so that plants are spaced 8 to 12 inches within the row.

HARVESTING

To keep kale productive, harvest lower leaves and remove any that have yellowed. Small, tender leaves can be used in salads. The flavor of most varieties becomes sweeter with the coming of fall. In all but the coldest areas you should be able to continue picking kale throughout the winter, with a flush of new growth just as the new year begins to warm up. Nip the flower buds for sautéing as they appear and wait for the new, tender leaves to come along.

SAVING SEEDS

Kale cross-pollinates readily with any member of the brassica family—broccoli, brussels sprouts, collards—that are within a thousand-foot bee's flight. Only a kale fanatic would seek that much isolation for the sake of this vegetable; a more practical alternative is to provide a barrier, such as a row of tall plants or your house itself, between kale and its cousins. Allow at least three plants to overwinter so that these self-sterile plants will have a community with which to share pollen. Pick the browned seed pods before they turn brittle and spill their contents.

red russian

VARIETIES

Lacinato. The hue and contours of this Italian heirloom's leaves set it apart, as does the chewy texture. Lacinato is tolerant of weather extremes.

Red Russian. This variety did indeed originate in Russia, and traveled through Canada to the United States. Along the way it picked up the alternative names Canadian Broccoli and Ragged Jack. The flavor is noticeably sweet even before frosts nip the plants. Red ribs contrast nicely with the cool grayish blue green of the leaves—Red Russian looks like a photograph that is badly (or wonderfully) in need of color correction. Young leaves add interest to mesclun mixes and salads.

Verdura. The compact, tender Verdura comes from the Netherlands. It is especially sweet, and can be harvested through the fall.

White Russian. This variation of Red Russian offers less color, but is especially mild and has less trouble with cold weather.

Wild Red. An unstable strain of kale produced this lavender-ribbed leaf, one among many variations.

white russian

lacinato

QUICK KALE STEW

SERVES 4 OR 5

Caldo Verde, the Portuguese soup based on kale and potatoes, has a rather thin consistency if made without the traditional chorizo sausage and a lot of olive oil. Here is a spin-off: The kale is steamed, then pureed; only a little water or stock is used; and ricotta makes this stew rich and substantial enough for a main dish. This is a good recipe in which to star small heirloom potatoes (see page 123)—you'll really be able to appreciate their flavor and texture as prepared here.

A nondairy stew can be made by replacing the ricotta with a pound of tofu, cut into cubes and lightly browned in the oil as you sauté the garlic.

½ pound kale

1 carrot, grated

5 to 6 cups fingerling potatoes, cut into ¾-inch lengths

3 tablespoons olive oil

5 cloves garlic, sliced

3 tablespoons balsamic vinegar

2 teaspoons salt

1 teaspoon ground black pepper

1 cup part-skim ricotta

Strip the stems from the kale leaves and chop them. Steam the kale and grated carrot until the kale is just tender, about 5 minutes. Set aside. Steam the potatoes until tender but still firm, about 10 minutes.

Sauté the garlic in the olive oil in a large skillet until just golden. Add the potatoes, vinegar, salt, and pepper and cook for 3 minutes, stirring occasionally. Roughly puree the kale and carrots in a food processor. Add the puree and the ricotta to the skillet and mix very well, coating the potatoes evenly. Cover and simmer for 10 minutes. If the stew appears too dry, stir in a few tablespoons of water. Serve hot.

GREEK DEEP-DISH CREPE

*This is something like spanokopita, but without the bother of phyllo. The crepe,
if you can call it that, forms itself around the edges of the baking dish. In other words,
the recipe, when served, seems like more trouble than it was.*

Olive oil
¼ cup bread crumbs
3 scallions, chopped
3 cloves garlic, minced
6 cups chopped kale or other greens,
   such as chard or mustard greens
½ cup minced dill
1 cup crumbled feta cheese
½ cup chopped parsley
1 large egg
3 large egg whites

Juice of 1 lemon
¼ teaspoon grated nutmeg
½ teaspoon salt
½ teaspoon ground black pepper

CREPE BATTER

1 large egg
1 large egg white
⅔ cup unbleached all-purpose flour
⅔ cup milk
¼ teaspoon salt

Preheat the oven to 350 degrees F.

Lightly oil 9-inch-square baking dish and cover the bottom with bread crumbs.

Sauté the scallions and garlic in 1 tablespoon olive oil in a large skillet. Add the
kale and cook until wilted, about 5 minutes. Remove from the heat. In a mixing
bowl, combine the greens, dill, feta, parsley, eggs, lemon juice, nutmeg, salt, and
pepper. Mix well. Spread the greens mixture evenly in the baking dish.

Thoroughly mix the ingredients for the crepe batter in a blender, and pour over
the greens. Let the batter run down at the edges to form an attractive crepelike
border all around the greens. Bake for 1 hour, or until set and lightly browned.

These are heirlooms that manage the neat trick of looking futuristic. In fact, kohlrabi is a modern development, relative to other garden crops, with a recorded history going back less than five hundred years.

Our parochialism about edibles and ornamentals keeps us from appreciating the colors, shapes, textures, and sheer scale of kohlrabi. True, when shorn of leaves it is the uncontested oddball of the produce department. But in the garden, kohlrabi's mantle of waxy leaves gives

KOHLRABI

it a grace all its own. The purple variety is particularly stunning, and at certain times of day it seems to glow with an inner light.

Kohlrabi tastes like a sweet cross of turnip and cabbage and is eaten either raw or cooked. It can be sliced, grated, or julienned. Kohlrabi keeps for a time in the refrigerator but otherwise may quickly lose its crispness after harvest. And crispness is key to enjoying it raw, as a crudité or in salads.

early white vienna

gigante

early purple vienna

GROWING

Hot weather doesn't suit kohlrabi; gardeners in warmer areas should plan on spring and fall crops. If your summers are cool, consider plantings every couple of weeks through the growing season for an ongoing harvest.

You can start seeds several weeks before the last spring frost date. Seeds should be ¼ inch deep. Set the plants out at a spacing of 6 inches, in rows 12 to 18 inches apart. Or sow directly in the garden near the last frost date with 1-inch spacing. (When you pull young, bulbless plants to achieve the 6-inch breathing room, try steaming whole and serving with oil and vinegar.) Eight to ten weeks before the first anticipated frost of fall, sow seeds for a late harvest.

HARVESTING

Gardening books and cookbooks routinely warn that kohlrabi will turn tough and unappealing if harvested when larger than a walnut. But don't despair if globes exceed that size before you get to them; they may still be crisp and sweet if the weather hasn't been terribly hot. A second crop will weather frosts and can be harvested on into the fall.

SAVING SEEDS

To save seeds from this biennial, mulch plants over winter. Or store the bulbs, with roots, in moist sand and set them out to flower a second season.

VARIETIES

Early Purple Vienna. Both purple and white Viennas were introduced before the 1860s, presumably from Austria. They continue to be widely available commercially and can be found on home-and-garden store seed racks each spring. The flesh inside the purple globe is white and tastes similar to White Vienna. For a stunning display in the garden, plant a row of purple kohlrabi alongside a row of Rainbow Swiss chard. Both crops offer the contrast of riotously colored ribs with cool blue-green foliage.

Early White Vienna. This is a pale-green twin of Early Purple, growing to harvestable size a few days earlier. It was the standard garden variety a century ago, and remains the most often planted.

Gigante. Introduced commercially by Southern Exposure Seed Exchange, this is an heirloom from eastern Europe, where it has been grated and processed in the manner of sauerkraut. As its name suggests, the stout-stemmed Gigante can grow to great sizes— routinely to 10 pounds, with a record of more than 60. The flavor and texture remain excellent through the season, making this variety an exception among kohlrabi.

Gigante seems resistant to root maggots and is worth a try if these pests have been a problem. It has a long growing season, with spring-planted seed yielding a fall crop. To overwinter plants in milder climates, set out seedlings in fall and protect with a generous layer of mulch.

GRILLED VEGETABLE LASAGNA

SERVES 6

Kohlrabi is one of several vegetables in this midsummer two-step dish. You roast the veggies on the grill one day, using the heat from a charcoal fire that has just cooked your dinner, and can assemble the lasagna a day or two later. It's a white lasagna because tomato sauce might obscure the delicate smoky flavor of the grilled ingredients.

MARINADE

2 tablespoons olive oil

2 tablespoons tamari

3 cloves garlic, finely minced

VEGETABLES

3 kohlrabi, julienned

2 beets, julienned

2 medium zucchini, cut lengthwise
   into ½-inch-thick slices

2 red bell peppers, halved

2 medium eggplants

ASSEMBLY

9 lasagna noodles

3 tablespoons olive oil

1 pound part-skim ricotta cheese

8 ounces tofu, mashed,
   or an additional 8 ounces ricotta

½ pound mozzarella cheese,
   shredded

2 tablespoons finely chopped basil

2 tablespoons balsamic vinegar

2 tablespoons grated asiago or
   romano cheese

Combine the olive oil, tamari, and garlic in a medium bowl. Add the kohlrabi, beets, zucchini, and peppers and toss to coat all the pieces. Form two low-sided dishes of aluminum foil in which to cook the kohlrabi and beets. Prick the skin of the eggplants in several places with a fork and wrap them in aluminum foil.

Place all the vegetables on the grill—the zucchini, peppers, and wrapped eggplant directly on the rack, and the kohlrabi and beets in their dishes. The zucchini and peppers need the closest attention; turn them to cook both sides, then remove from the grill. Test the kohlrabi and beets for tenderness with a fork. The eggplants will take longer than the rest. Rotate them after 15 minutes so that they cook evenly. After 30 minutes, begin pressing the foil to find if the insides have softened. When they have, remove the eggplants from the heat.

Allow the eggplants to cool somewhat, then unwrap. Cut them in half, scoop out the insides, and mash with a fork or potato masher. Dice the zucchini and

peppers. Place the vegetables in a bowl, cover, and refrigerate until time to complete the recipe.

When ready to assemble the lasagna, preheat the oven to 350 degrees F.

Cook 9 lasagna noodles in boiling salted water until al dente. Spread 1 tablespoon of the olive oil in a 9-x-13-inch baking dish and place 3 noodles over the bottom. Combine the ricotta, tofu, mozzarella, and basil and spread half of this mixture over the noodles. Add the vinegar to the bowl of vegetables, stir well, and spread somewhat less than half over the ricotta mixture.

Put down another 3 noodles, followed by the remaining ricotta mixture and all but several tablespoons of the vegetables. Put down the final 3 noodles and scatter the remaining vegetables over the top like confetti. Drizzle the remaining 2 tablespoons olive oil and sprinkle the grated cheese over the top. Cover with aluminum foil.

Bake for 40 minutes, turn off the oven, and let the dish sit in the cooling oven for another 15 minutes before serving.

BRILLIANT JULIENNED KOHLRABI

SERVES 4 TO 6

*In this colorful recipe, kohlrabi's plain white canvas is dyed to shocking
pastels by the close company of beets.*

2 cups julienned kohlrabi	1 tablespoon olive oil
1 cup julienned beets	½ teaspoon salt
1 cup julienned carrots	1 tablespoon finely chopped basil
1 tablespoon red wine vinegar	

Steam the kohlrabi, beets, and carrots in a basket over boiling water for 8 minutes. Transfer to a serving bowl and toss until they are thoroughly mixed. Cover and refrigerate for at least 4 hours.

Prepare a dressing with the vinegar, oil, and salt and toss the vegetables with it just before serving. Sprinkle chopped basil over each portion.

Lettuce is climbing out of a slough of indifference, thanks in part to the interest in heirloom varieties. The cool, bland dominance of iceberg and romaine has been challenged by dozens of multicolored, idiosyncratic lettuces bred over the centuries and gaining new converts.

LETTUCE

Lettuces are corralled under terms having to do with their form. Looseleaf varieties grow informal, somewhat floppy heads from which individual leaves can be harvested; for this reason they are also called cutting lettuce. Considered the easiest of lettuces to grow, looseleafs include many old and colorful varieties. Of the heading varieties, the butterheads (including bibb and Boston lettuces) form delicate, ruffled heads; they are nearly as foolproof as looseleaf varieties, and less prone to bolting. And crispheads are more challenging to grow, needing more time to mature, but bolting is less likely to be a problem with them. Finally, romaine or cos lettuces have long, upright leaves, an attitude that conserves space in the garden.

beginning. To protect plants from freezing temperatures, use floating row covers or plastic tunnels, available from mail-order seed companies and some nurseries. Consider planting heirlooms that are known for performing well at the onset of winter weather.

GROWING

Lettuce takes to cool weather, 65 degrees F. and down. That holds for all types, but warmth is less apt to interfere with romaine and crisphead varieties.

Begin sowing seeds indoors in flats three to four weeks before the last frost date, 1 to 2 inches apart. Don't allow sunlight to warm the soil above 75 degrees. Two or three days before transplanting the seedlings, harden them off by lowering the temperature. Space transplants 8 to 12 inches apart within rows, and rows 12 to 18 inches apart.

In the garden, you can begin direct sowing successive plantings as soon as the soil can be worked. Sow seeds 1 inch apart and cover with ⅛ inch of fine soil, patting it down as you go. Stop sowing when summer gets under way in earnest; once soil temperatures rise to 70 degrees or so, the seeds are programmed to wait for cool weather to return before germinating. To keep lettuce rows cooler, arrange them to take advantage of shade from taller crops—pole beans, tomatoes, or corn.

Mid-July and August plantings of lettuce will be spared the worst of summer's heat and yield a second season of salads until after frost. You can start them in flats or small pots, repeating the early spring ritual—only now the objective is to give them a cool, shaded

HARVESTING

Young leaves are the most tender and least apt to be bitter; and by continually picking the young leaves, you discourage plants from bolting as summer temperatures climb. Lettuce is at its best if picked early in the morning, when still cool and dewy from the night, or just before giving it a whirl in the salad spinner at the dinner hour. For mesclun salads, get into the habit of taking a pair of scissors into the garden every day or two and mowing greens that are just 4 or 5 inches high; if not harvested too severely, the plants should continue to grow.

SAVING SEEDS

Because lettuce self-pollinates, you don't have to worry much about errant crosses. Yank any wild lettuces that happen to be lurking on the grounds to avoid their involvement; consult a wildflower field guide to identify them. After the yellow flowers have turned into fluffy, white seed heads, remove the seeds and take them indoors to dry.

LOOSELEAF

Bronze Arrow. The especially attractive leaves have an excellent, mild flavor. Plants are slow to bolt in warm spells and may survive winter snows.

Deer Tongue. Modern texts continue to describe this 1740s heirloom as looking like a green deer's tongue, a field mark that must mean little to most gardeners. (Still more obscure is an heirloom lettuce named for its supposed resemblance to canary tongues.) Call them spearhead-shape leaves. They form an attractive, compact rosette—you can arrange the heads (with roots) in bowls of water as an edible centerpiece that keeps the lettuce fresh for days.

Red Oak Leaf. Lettuce varieties with leaves shaped like those of an oak have been known for more than three hundred years. This one responds to sunlight by producing various shades of red, depending on conditions, making it a good companion to the standard Green Oak Leaf. It can manage warmer weather without bolting or turning bitter and eases into cool fall weather as well. Shepherd's Garden Seeds names this the most popular variety among growers who supply the gourmet restaurant trade. Seeds of Change notes that Red Oak performs especially well in the Pacific Northwest.

bronze arrow

deer tongue

red oak leaf

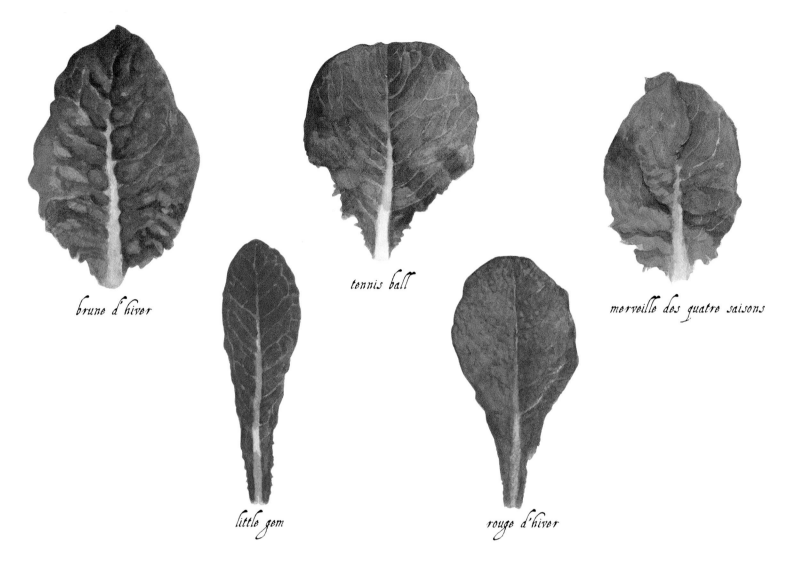

brune d'hiver

tennis ball

merveille des quatre saisons

little gem

rouge d'hiver

HEADING

Brune d'Hiver. As the name suggests, this French lettuce from the 1850s can handle cold weather. Low temperatures add a reddish hue to the bronzed leaves.

Merveille des Quatre Saisons. Also labeled as Four Seasons, this French variety's leaves are accented with red, contrasting with light green at the heart. Merveille is one of the best-known French heirlooms, suited to spring and late-season crops.

Tennis Ball. This small bibb lettuce was grown by Thomas Jefferson at Monticello, and dates to before 1804. It is best suited for planting in early spring.

ROMAINE (COS)

Little Gem. Known also as Suchrine, Little Gem is easy to grow and produces over a long period. Garden City Seeds of Hamilton, Montana, recommends it for children's gardens.

french arugula

osaka purple

merveille des quatre saisons

rainbow chard

red treviso

seven-top turnip

russian kale

corn salad

Rouge d'Hiver. A lovely French variety from before 1850, Rouge d'Hiver is valued for weathering cold, season-end temperatures. The leaves have a buttery texture and sweet flavor.

MESCLUN

Mesclun is the French term (*misticanza*, in Italian) for a mix of various greens harvested young. The lines of seedlings look like miniature hedgerows, with their many variations on green and red and their distinctive profiles. Mesclun may seem to be a faddish restaurant item, but it's really just a twist on a very old practice—snipping spring greens soon after they nose above ground.

The year's first leafy things have been regarded as a tonic by many cultures over the centuries. In Pennsylvania Dutch country, good health would be yours in the year ahead if you ate spring greens on Maundy Thursday, the Thursday before Easter. The Greeks stalk whatever wild spring greens they can

EDIBLE FLOWERS

For a pointillistic effect,
toss flower blossoms
into salads. A few choices
to keep in mind on
your strolls around the
yard are bergamot, chive,
dianthus, hollyhocks,
marigold (in moderation),
nasturtium, pea,
runner beans, and violet.

find to make Hortopita (page 95), a zippier version of *spanokopita*. In parts of North America, dandelion foraging is still a rite of spring.

Mesclun formalizes the foraging process. You sow a mix of greens, spicy and mild, tender and a bit toothsome. Some gardeners use a seed company's formulation, while others prefer to come up with their own balance. Douglas Hendrickson, a Washington State market gardener who grows on contract for a number of subscribing households, makes a mix that might include kale, chard, beet leaves, Asian greens, baby spinach, and wild mustards. The first response from several customers was "Where's the lettuce?", but they have come to look forward to the full-flavored blends.

Buy enough seeds for successive planting in spring and as summer temperatures moderate. Several mesclun ingredients are illustrated here. All are described in this chapter or elsewhere in the book, except for corn salad, or mâche, a delicate European favorite with a faintly nutty flavor.

SALAD DRESSING

Store-bought bottled dressings don't do justice to homegrown greens.
Oil and vinegar, spiked with garlic, are all you need.

For a salad serving four, combine 1 tablespoon olive oil, 2 tablespoons red wine or balsamic vinegar, 1 minced garlic clove, and salt to taste. If possible, let the dressing sit for at least half an hour so that the garlic can suffuse the liquid.

As a change, mix up dressing for four from 1 tablespoon *each* tahini (sesame butter), lemon juice, and tamari.

INVOLTINI DI LATTUGA

SERVES 6

Don't be put off by the prospect of eating cooked lettuce. Occasionally
a few ordinary ingredients will combine in a simple dish to suggest other flavors.
Here is an example of that synergy.

½ onion, chopped
1 tablespoon olive oil
2 cups tomato sauce
6 ounces provolone cheese, shredded

1 large egg, beaten
¾ cup bread crumbs
12 large romaine or cos leaves

Preheat the oven to 375 degrees F.

Sauté the onions in the olive oil in a medium saucepan until translucent, about 5 minutes. Add the tomato sauce and simmer, partially covered, for 10 minutes. Mix the provolone, egg, and bread crumbs. Set aside.

Select long, good-looking lettuce leaves and parboil them in a covered skillet with ½ inch of boiling water for 1 or 2 minutes. Remove the leaves and pat dry with paper towel. Position each leaf with the inside surface facing up and the base away from you, and spread a portion of the cheese mixture over it. Roll up the leaf from tip to base, and secure by passing a toothpick through the rib. Place the rolls in a baking dish and spoon the tomato sauce over them. Bake for 10 minutes. Serve hot.

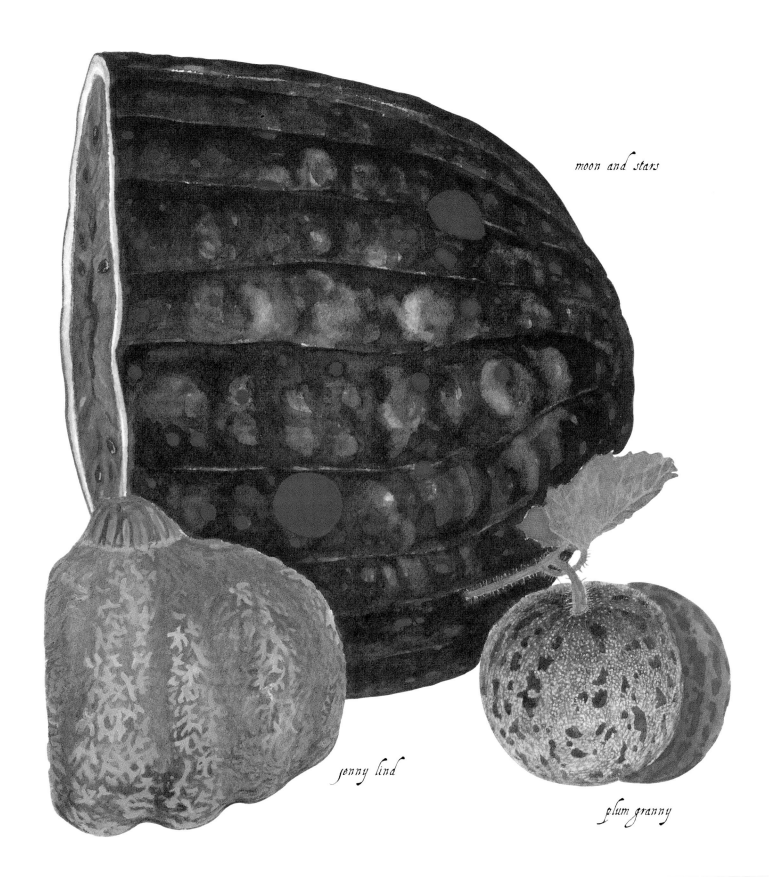

moon and stars

jenny lind

plum granny

Melon terminology is somewhat confusing. We tend to speak of both green-fleshed and orange-fleshed melons as cantaloupes, but both are properly called muskmelons and are distinguished by the netted rind. The true cantaloupe isn't often grown in the United States. Watermelons, although included here, are another genus altogether. Their flesh is indeed watery and ranges from yellow to orange and pinkish-red in color.

The memory of a superb melon can haunt a person for a lifetime. Many heirloom growers swap seeds in an

MELON AND WATERMELON

effort to find varieties that meet the standards—real or imagined—of a past summer. But the variety is only half the answer. The quality of each year's crop is highly dependent on growing conditions. Wet weather (or heavy watering) in the last three weeks before harvest can turn melons insipid.

GROWING

If your climate grants you at least 120 frostfree growing days, you can stick melon seeds right in the garden soil. Otherwise, sow indoors no more than a month before the last frost date, placing three or four seeds each in 3-inch pots, ¼ inch deep. Keep them between 80 and 90 degrees F. to encourage germination, moderating to 75 degrees once the plants come up. Further lower the temperature one week before setting out plants to harden them. After the frost date, when the soil has had a chance to warm, set three young plants per hill, spacing the hills 3 feet in one direction and 6 feet apart in the other. A garden bed that pitches to the south will help melons mature faster. Failing that, you can take advantage of the soil-warming effects of black plastic, placing it over the soil a week before bringing out the transplants. Floating row covers will shelter the young plants for their first month of outdoor life; remove them when you see female blossoms, identified by a swelling at the base.

Although a good supply of moisture is important to early development, melons will be at their best if you cut back on watering in the last two weeks before the anticipated harvest.

HARVESTING

Use the fragrance test to determine when cantaloupes are ready to be harvested; they won't ripen and sweeten further after having been cut. Or, give a poke where stem meets fruit, and a ripe cantaloupe will begin to come free. A yellowing of the rind is the sign that honeydews should be cut from the vine; they'll be ready to eat when they've further ripened indoors for a few days, at which point you'll pick up their characteristic scent. The time-honored way to judge a ripe watermelon is to thump it with the knuckles and listen for a low, hollow "punk" sound; if the watermelon responds with a "pink," it needs more time.

SAVING SEEDS

Melons will cross with melons, but not with their cuke, squash, and pumpkin relatives. To maintain a variety as is, isolate plants at least 200 feet, or pollinate by hand (see page 137). The seeds are ready to be collected when a melon is ready to eat. Rinse them and dry on paper towel.

VARIETIES

Jenny Lind. Dating to before the Civil War, this Armenian native was named for a Swede, the wildly popular singer Jenny Lind, who toured the United States in the mid-1800s. (Less flattering, a huge potato fit only for livestock also shared her name.) The pale green flesh is sweet and aromatic. A relatively short growing season suits it to gardeners in cooler zones.

Plum Granny. It seems that these curious melons were once grown to be smelled, not eaten. Old sources say they were tucked into clothing to mask body odor—hence its British name, Queen Anne's Pocket Melon. But the Granny is very edible, if a trifle bland,

and the cheery little fruits are gemlike conversation pieces for the garden, flower beds, or porch trellises. The delicate vines won't overtake garden beds and can be tucked almost anywhere. They take no coddling to produce a good crop. The reptilian patterning of the faintly fuzzy fruits will turn from a two-tone green to an orangey gold as a signal the grannies are ripe.

Moon and Stars. A star among heirlooms, this is far and away the most popular watermelon offered by members of Seed Savers Exchange. The evocative name doesn't hurt; it describes, a little fancifully, the spattering of bright yellow dots in a firmament of deep green. The flavorful pinkish-red flesh is another reason for the melon's renown. And then there's the dramatic story of its rediscovery in the 1980s. Missouri gardener Merle Van Doren alerted Seed Savers that he still had seeds for what had been a well-known commercial variety sixty years before and was now considered extinct. There is also a yellow-fleshed variety, slightly less sweet in flavor, from seed held by a family in Georgia.

THE MELON CHALLENGE

For many gardeners, producing a successful melon crop is the crowning achievement of the season. Melons taste and look somewhat tropical and seem exotic next to standard row crops. But their sprawling, sun-loving nature can be discouraging. If your space is limited, look for compact varieties. And if heat is in short supply, choose a quick-maturing melon.

MOON AND STARS WATERMELON SOUP

At summer's end, this cool soup is whipped up by chef Michael Geary
of the Farmhouse Restaurant in Emmaus, Pennsylvania. Any variety of watermelon
will do, but Moon and Stars is an eye-catcher on the menu and
a conversation starter around the dinner table. To prepare a simple syrup,
dissolve 1 cup sugar in ½ cup boiling water. Let cool before serving.
Refrigerate any surplus.

4 cups cut-up watermelon flesh,   ½ cup simple syrup
  seeded   Juice and zest of 1 lemon
1 cup plain yogurt

Puree all ingredients in a blender. Chill before serving.

MELON BALL SALAD

Ripe melons can't be improved upon in the kitchen. But it's fun to experiment
with their cool, subtle flavors in summer recipes. Sue Gronholz, a market gardener
from Columbus, Wisconsin, uses an aromatic dressing to turn a melon
ball salad into something curious, even exotic.

½ cup sugar   1 teaspoon chopped mint leaves
Dash of salt   1 teaspoon chopped anise
1 cup warm water   hyssop leaves
3 tablespoons lime juice   Melon balls

Dissolve ½ cup sugar and a dash of salt in 1 cup warm water. Add 3 tablespoons lime juice, 1 teaspoon chopped mint leaves, and 1 teaspoon chopped anise hyssop leaves. (Anise hyssop is a hauntingly scented member of the mint family, with a lingering sweet taste. It is easily grown from seed and offers the ornament of white or purple blossoms. If you don't have any on hand, just double the amount of chopped mint leaves.) Allow the dressing to steep for 2 hours. Prepare the melon balls by scooping with either the utensil made for that purpose or a small spoon. Pour on the dressing through a strainer to remove the leaves. Mix well.

PLUM GRANNY GELATIN

SERVES 4

This is a light dessert, fragrant and perfumed, with just the right balance between sweet and sour. It is based on a recipe suggested by Nancy M. Grant of Ohio, a woman so fond of the little melons that her address labels identify her as the Friendship Plum Granny Gardener. You can substitute other melons for the Grannies, using ½ to 1 cup of pulp.

4 Plum Grannies

Juice of 1 lime

1 cup cider without preservatives

2 tablespoons sugar

1 tablespoon unflavored gelatin

Halve the melons and remove the seeds. Use a teaspoon to scoop out the pulp from the skin. Put the pulp in a blender jar, add the lime juice and ½ cup of the cider, and blend. Heat the remaining cider in a small saucepan to not quite boiling and stir in the sugar and gelatin until dissolved. Stir in the melon mixture and pour into 4 sherbet glasses. Refrigerate until firm.

serifon

osaka purple

red giant

These Asian mustards are grown for their leaves. And they grow enthusiastically, yielding a profusion of flavorful greens for stir-fries or spur-of-the-moment sautéing for sandwiches, omelets, and side dishes. Picked young (before their

MUSTARD GREENS

flavor has grown teeth), the leaves can be added to salads. With the new interest in Asian cuisines, seeds for many mustard varieties have become available.

GROWING

Mustards need little care and take off quickly. Plant seeds in the garden in early spring and again in mid- to late summer. The later sowing will be less prone to bolting. Sow ¼ to ½ inch deep, a dozen seeds to the foot, in rows 2 feet apart. Thin to allow at least 6 inches between plants.

HARVESTING

Start snipping young leaves for salads. Leaves 6 inches or longer are better used in stir-fries. Keep snipping, because soon enough the plants will flower (you can snip and eat the buds) and go to seed, getting stronger flavored by the minute. These mustards also can be mowed with scissors at the seedling stage as part of a mesclun mix.

VARIETIES

Osaka Purple. A glorious sight in the garden, Osaka is easy to grow. If you allow seed heads of spring-sown plants to flower, you can expect a volunteer fall crop scattered among beds and garden paths. The flavor is bracing in salads, and Osaka is excellent either steamed or sautéed.

Red Giant. And a giant it is, if allowed to grow, with a spreading form. The purpley, sun-bronzed tops of the leaves contrast with the cool-green of the undersides and shaded smaller leaves. A yellow, barely perfumed flower appears on a tall stalk. The leaves make a visual splash when mixed with lettuce in salads, and the flavor is not overly assertive if leaves are harvested when no longer than 6 inches.

Serifon. A more delicately constructed variety, Serifon or Serifong is only mildly mustardy when young, but older leaves become aggressively hot. The name is an adaptation of the Mandarin for "stem in the snow," leading to the alternate Western name of Green-in-the-Snow mustard.

HORTOPITA

MAKES 16 HORTOPITA

*This is an untamed version of the Greek spinach-filled spanokopita,
combining mustard greens with anything you can scrounge from the garden. Note that
you should not harvest greens from a lawn or roadside that has been treated
with chemical pesticides, herbicides, or fertilizer.*

¼ cup olive oil

1 cup chopped sweet onion

6 cups chopped mustard and mixed
   spring greens

½ cup grated asiago or crumbled
   feta cheese

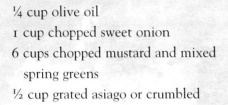

10 to 12 kalamata olives,
   pitted and slivered

2 tablespoons lemon juice

½ teaspoon ground black pepper

12 sheets phyllo

Heat 1 tablespoon of the oil in a saucepan and sauté the chopped onion until
translucent, about 5 minutes. Add the chopped greens and stir until wilted, also about
5 minutes. Empty the saucepan into a mixing bowl and stir in the cheese, olives,
lemon juice, and black pepper. Set aside.

Preheat the oven to 375 degrees F. Lightly coat a baking sheet with olive oil.
Unfold the sheets of phyllo and stack them on the work surface. Cover the stack with
a clean, slightly dampened dish towel so that the phyllo sheets do not dry out as you
work. Remove a sheet of phyllo from the stack and place it on the countertop before
you, long sides to the left and right. Dip a pastry brush in the remaining 3 tablespoons
of oil and lightly paint the sheet. Place another sheet squarely on top and brush again;
add a third sheet and brush that as well. Use a sharp knife to make 3 lengthwise cuts,
forming 4 long stacks of strips. Evenly distribute 3 level tablespoons of the greens
mixture over the closer half of each of the top strips, spreading it in a thin layer.

To fold the phyllo strips into the distinctive triangular shape, begin by lifting the
right bottom corner of a strip and folding it on the diagonal to make a triangle with 2
legs of equal length. Next, lift the triangle point closest to you and fold it over, like
folding a flag. Continue folding triangles until you reach the end of the strip. Place
on the baking sheet. When all 4 strips have been folded and placed on the baking
sheet, repeat the same procedure with the remaining phyllo sheets.

Bake for 20 minutes, or until the phyllo has deepened slightly in color. Serve
either hot out of the oven or when cooled to room temperature.

If there's a National Board of Okra Growers, you can bet that mucilaginous is a dirty word in their offices. Okra does have that quality about it, and there is no  appetizing way to describe the mouthfeel of the vegetable. But okra lovers get around this slight character flaw by frying to change the texture or by using the vegetable to thicken stews (most famously, gumbos) and cooked beans.

The plants produce large, showy blossoms of a creamy yellow, marked by a maroon center. They look like hollyhock or hibiscus flowers, and these plants are in fact okra's relatives.

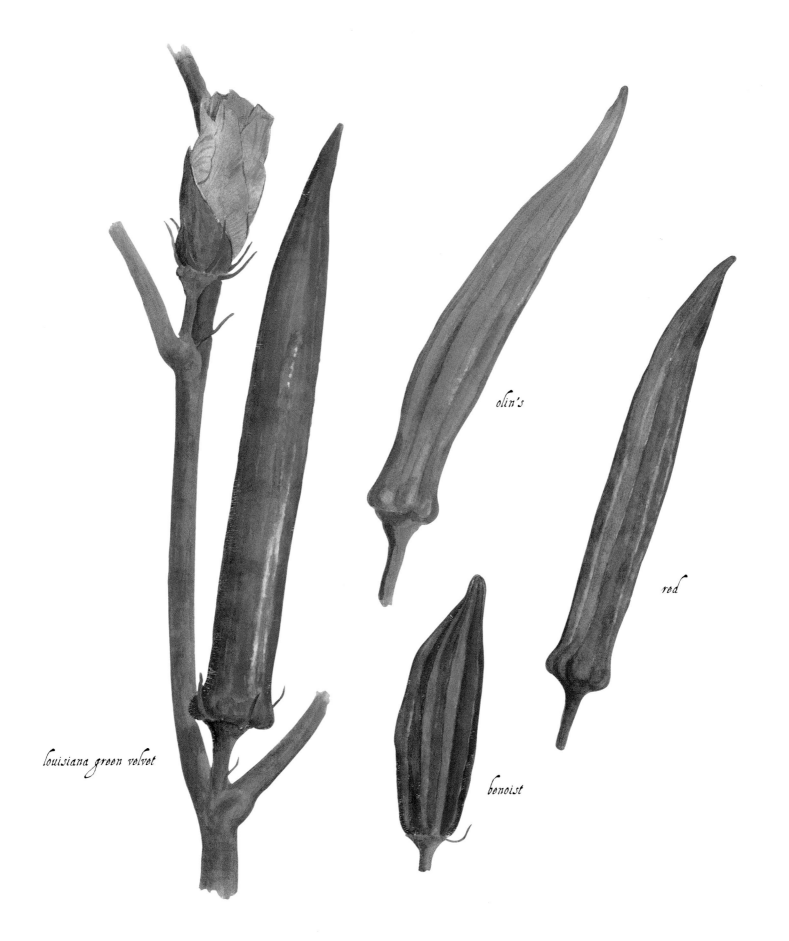

louisiana green velvet

olin's

red

benoist

GROWING

In the North, start seeds indoors, ½ inch deep about 4 weeks before the last frost. Encourage germination with bottom heat of 80 to 90 degrees F. Plant out seedlings 12 to 18 inches apart, in rows 24 inches apart. In warmer climates, you can direct seed once the soil has reached the mid 60s.

HARVESTING

For best flavor and texture, harvest the pods when no more than 3 inches long, before they grow into dangerous-looking projectiles.

SAVING SEEDS

After selecting plants you want to sire next year's crop, allow some of their pods to stay on until the end of the season to ripen. After removing the seeds, allow them to dry for a week before storing.

VARIETIES

Benoist. This blunt okra is said to have been in the Benoist family of Mississippi for more than a century.

Louisiana Green Velvet. The pods of this okra are long and tender, and rated the best of twenty varieties grown by Seed Savers Exchange member Carol Hillhouse of California.

Olin's. You aren't apt to find this one in commercial seed catalogs, at least not for some time. It is a backyard favorite in Georgia, named for a gardener in that state and valued for its fine flavor.

Red. Also known as Purple okra, this decorative variety can handle hot, dry spells. The pods stay tender longer than most.

OKRA TIPS

Ask heirloom gardeners around the country for their favorite family okra recipes, and you get variations— slight ones—on breading and frying. Stephen D. Posey, a Georgia gardener, likes to add a little ground coriander to the cornmeal and flour he uses for breading; he serves the fried okra with malt vinegar. Another tip, if you're troubled by okra's mouthfeel, is to take the extra step of baking the rounds after frying them.

LADY FINGERS IN YOGURT

Indian cuisine meets okra head on, using it in full-flavored curries and even boiling and mashing it with mustard oil. Okra dishes are known in India as bhindi or, in a whimsical leftover from the British raj, as lady fingers. This dish is to be accompanied by rice.

1 pound okra

4 tablespoons butter or vegetable oil

2 onions, finely chopped

2 cloves garlic, minced

½ teaspoon ground coriander

½ teaspoon turmeric

½ teaspoon ground cumin

¼ teaspoon ground cloves

½ teaspoon salt

1 cup plain yogurt

Hot cooked rice, for serving

Cilantro leaves, for garnish

Cut the okra into rounds and fry in the butter in a large skillet until slightly browned, about 10 minutes. Set aside. Using the same pan, sauté the onions and garlic. Add the spices and salt and cook for 5 minutes, stirring often. Stir in the yogurt, cover, and cook for 5 minutes more. Add 1 or 2 tablespoons water if the mixture appears to be drying out. Return the okra to the pan and continue to cook until hot, about 5 minutes. Serve with the rice. Garnish with the cilantro leaves.

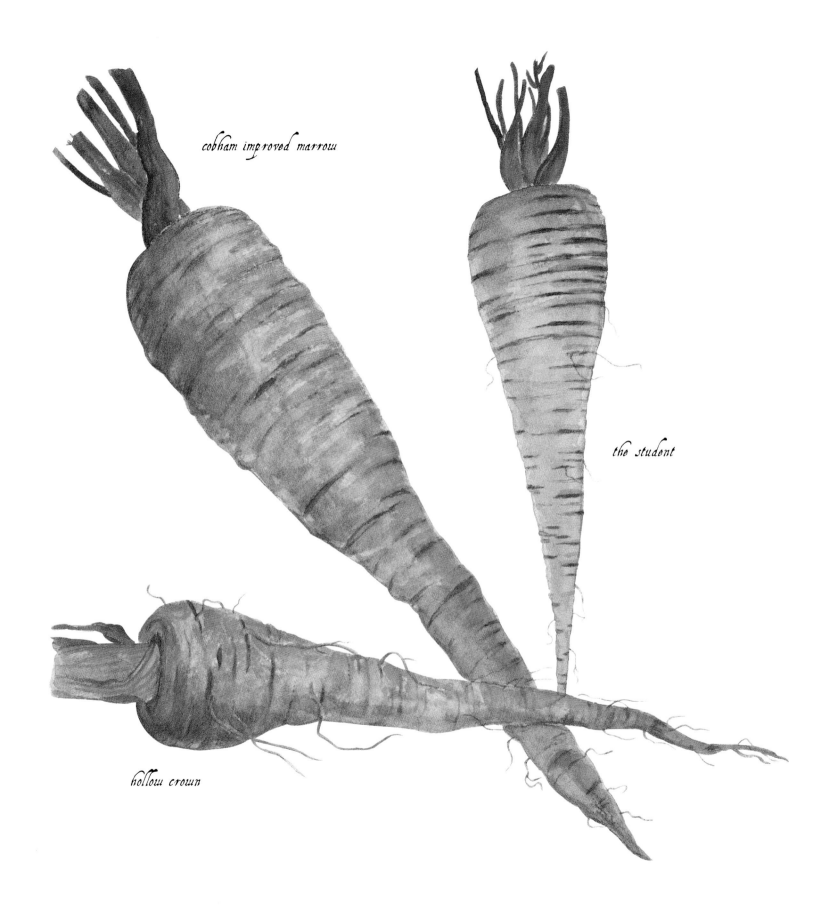

cobham improved marrow

the student

hollow crown

A century ago, when gardening writers didn't feel called upon to promote their topic, an author could get away with a remark like this: "Everybody grows parsnips, so far as I can make out, and hardly anyone ever eats them." So said Maria Theresa Earle in her how-to book, *More Pot-Pourri from a Surrey Garden*, published in 1899. Parsnips are treated

PARSNIPS

by both gardening books and gardeners as one of the minor vegetables, but they do inspire something like devotion among those who have figured out how to grow them well. As a member of the parsley family, parsnips have a similar clean, herbal taste, with more complexity than carrots. In fact, it is probably because parsnips are dismissed as pale-complected carrots that they aren't used more often.

GROWING

Parsnips take patience. To begin with, seeds must be fresh if you are to have a good germination percentage. The seeds seem to take forever to rouse themselves— three weeks. And the soil must be deeply worked if they are to do well. Plant seeds in the garden in early spring to mid-spring, ½ inch deep and 1 inch apart in rows spaced 18 to 24 inches. Mist the seed bed as needed and thin seedlings to an in-row spacing of 4 inches. Gardeners in warmer zones can plant in fall for harvesting in spring.

HARVESTING

Parsnips become sweeter if left in the ground through hard fall frosts and can even be mulched and allowed to remain until early the following spring. But these biennials must be pulled before they enter their sopho-more phase of flowering, or the roots will turn woody.

SAVING SEEDS

The commercial viability of many parsnip varieties is precarious, adding incentive to collect their seeds— several heirlooms exist only through the efforts of gardeners. Allow the roots to overwinter and begin growing again the following spring. After they bolt and flower, gather the drying tops and bring them indoors to dry completely so that the seeds won't scatter. Unless you have two gardens a good distance apart, concentrate on perpetuating a single variety—parsnips will cross-pollinate. Seeds are viable for just one year.

VARIETIES

Cobham Improved Marrow. Wisconsin gardener Wayne Jeidy has been selecting seed from this variety for years to improve it a little further. The roots are long, slender, and uniform, with attractive tops; the sweet taste has been likened to coconut, once frosts have worked their alchemy on the roots.

Hollow Crown. The name refers to the dished, or dented, top end. Hollow Crown has been a standard garden variety for many decades.

The Student. The curious name may be explained by the fact that the man who developed this old variety was a teacher—Professor James Buckman of Britain's Royal Agricultural College. One of the few current North American sources of The Student, Howe Sound Seeds of British Columbia, tells the story in its catalog.

Buckman gathered seeds from wild turnips and sowed them in 1849. He then patiently worked with the best of that crop to develop The Student through 28 generations. This variety was credited with being the sweetest parsnip in cultivation, and it may have the pronounced aroma of lavender.

Richard Prince of Buffalo, New York, picked up seeds while in England and now grows The Student each year to make parsnip-ginger wine. Prince doesn't drink all of his harvest, though. He sautés the parsnips in butter until tender, deglazing with orange juice—a recipe difficult to improve upon.

Parsnip Tagine

*A tagine is a Moroccan dish akin to a stew but a lot better looking.
That's because the ingredients are arranged with care, not jumbled together,
and served from the distinctive clay pot in which they are cooked over
a period of hours. In Morocco, low-cost, handmade tagine pots are placed
over charcoal and allowed to simmer through the afternoon, their dunce-hat
lids trapping steam and flavors. The ingredients take on a smoky tang.*

*By the time a fragile tagine pot is wrapped and shipped to North America,
it is no longer inexpensive. (The pots are available from Sam's
Souk, 979 Lexington Ave., New York, NY 10021.) You can make do
with a large, heavy skillet topped with a steam-catching cap
fashioned from aluminum foil, a stockpot, or a stovetop casserole.*

2 large onions, chopped

6 parsnips, quartered lengthwise

2 zucchini, quartered lengthwise

2 carrots, quartered lengthwise

6 medium potatoes, cubed

2 turnips, cubed

1 rutabaga, cubed

1 teaspoon freshly grated ginger

½ teaspoon grated cinnamon

½ teaspoon ground cumin

½ teaspoon ground cardamom

½ teaspoon turmeric

½ teaspoon ground star anise

½ teaspoon ground black pepper

¼ teaspoon grated nutmeg

⅛ teaspoon saffron

1 teaspoon salt

3 tablespoons olive oil

12 cherry tomatoes

12 pitted prunes

12 kalamata olives

2 tablespoons wine vinegar

Juice of 1 lemon

1 lime, halved

2 tablespoons butter

½ cup whole almonds, toasted

Prepare the vegetables. Combine the ginger, the 8 spices listed after it, and the salt
in a bowl. Set aside. Coat the bottom of the pot with the olive oil. Make a layer of
the potatoes. To prevent the onions from blackening over the long cooking period,
mound them on top of the potatoes. Symmetrically assemble the prepared vegetables

in a low pyramid, sprinkling the dry spice mix over the ingredients as you go. If any quartered vegetables are too long to fit, cut them in the middle. Evenly distribute the cherry tomatoes, prunes, and olives over the pyramid.

Pour ¼ cup water over the top, followed by the vinegar, lemon juice, and juice of half a lime. Distribute pats of butter here and there. Perch the remaining lime half on top like the cherry on a sundae. Cover, and cook over very low heat for 4 to 6 hours, or until the root vegetables are entirely tender when poked with a fork. Look under the lid from time to time and add another ¼ cup water if the pot seems dry at the bottom. Toast the almonds and distribute them over the top of the *tagine* before serving. Any broth in the bottom of the pot can be spooned over the *tagine*. Serve hot.

Note: The ingredients of a tagine vary from one region of Morocco to another, taking advantage of local harvests. This recipe is accented by the almonds and prunes used in tagines of the mountainous area around Tafraoute, along with several root crops. Modify the ingredients list to take advantage of whatever you are harvesting. Serve with couscous and yogurt.

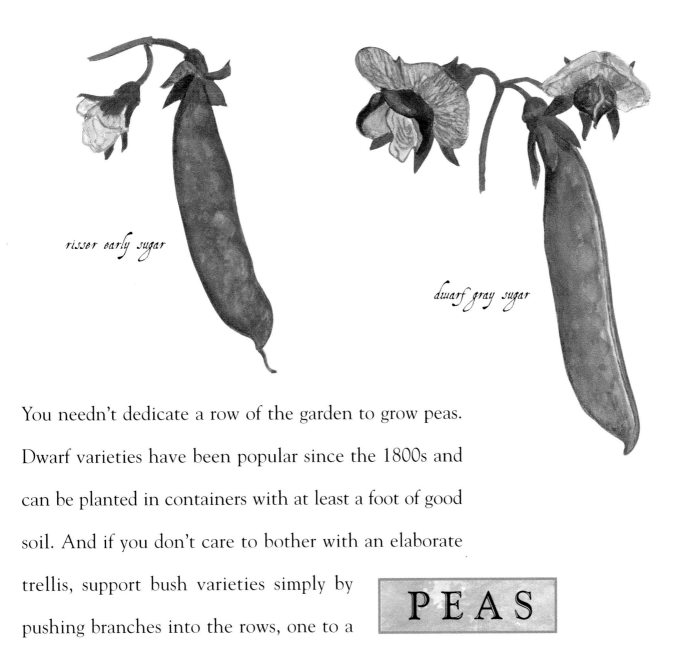

risser early sugar

dwarf gray sugar

You needn't dedicate a row of the garden to grow peas. Dwarf varieties have been popular since the 1800s and can be planted in containers with at least a foot of good soil. And if you don't care to bother with an elaborate trellis, support bush varieties simply by pushing branches into the rows, one to a plant. Advocates of gardening have no more eloquent argument than fresh-picked peas—a precious and perishable crop, losing sweetness by the moment, and not to be enjoyed at their peak unless grown nearby.

PEAS

dwarf telephone

lincoln

thomas laxton

little marvel

GROWING

Plan on two plantings, the first in early spring and the second two months before the fall frost date. Set seeds ½ to 1 inch deep and 1 to 1½ inches apart in 3-inch-wide strips. Row spacing depends on the type of pea: allow 12 to 18 inches for a dwarf variety, 4 to 6 inches if you will be using trellises. Do not thin. You can increase yields by treating either dampened seeds or the soil with a bacterial legume inoculant. Support vines with branches implanted in the ground or with trellises made by stretching wires between stakes, top and bottom, and running lengths of twine between the wires.

HARVESTING

The progress of shell peas can be monitored by the shape of the peas within the pods. Harvest daily, both to have peas at their best and to encourage production. Sugar or snow peas should be picked before they mature into starchy middle age.

SAVING SEEDS

Although peas won't cross-pollinate with other members of the pea family, they may with each other, even though blossoms are self-pollinating. Varieties from which you'll be saving seeds should be kept 50 feet apart, or 10 feet if separated by a tall barrier crop. To make sure the peas won't be damaged by dampness, gather the pods for a final drying undercover.

SHELLING

Dwarf Telephone. Plants grow to a couple of feet high and bring in a late harvest to extend the pea season. Dwarf Telephone was introduced in 1888.

Little Marvel. A dwarf vine, Little Marvel reaches just a foot-and-a-half tall, but yields are good and the peas mature over a fairly long period. The variety was developed in England in 1900, became available in North America eight years later, and remains one of the most popular garden peas.

Lincoln. The dwarf vines of the century-old Lincoln grow to 2 or 3 feet, and the yellow-green peas are wrinkled—an indication of sweetness.

Thomas Laxton. Commemorating a plant breeder, this variety appeared in North America in 1900. The vines are semidwarf, quickly reaching 3 feet in height.

SNOW (SUGAR)

Dwarf Gray Sugar. This popular pea dates to before the Revolution. It matures quickly, needing as little as two months before you can begin picking. The lilac blossoms are worth clipping and tucking into a tiny vase along with a few tendrils.

Risser Early Sugar. The Rissers, an Amish family of Lancaster County, Pennsylvania, originated this white-flowering pea. It is not yet carried by commercial seed companies.

MINTED PEAS IN TURNIP CUPS

*You can invite turnips to a dinner party with this quaint (but fussy) recipe,
adapted from Ida D. Bennett's* The Vegetable Garden, *published in 1908.
Fresh peas are served in cups made by hollowing out cooked turnips.*

8 small turnips (2-inch diameter)	1 teaspoon finely minced mint
1 cup fresh peas	¼ teaspoon salt
1 tablespoon butter	¼ teaspoon ground black pepper

Square off the bottoms and tops of the turnips; there is no need to peel them, and
the popular Purple Top White Globe variety will show off its color. Steam the
turnips until tender, about 30 minutes. Holding onto each with folded paper
toweling, use a paring or grapefruit knife to cut around the edges and a teaspoon to
scoop out the centers. Be careful to avoid poking through. (If the centers aren't soft
enough to remove easily, steam for another 5 to 10 minutes.) Simmer the peas with
the butter, mint, salt, pepper, and enough water to cover the bottom until tender.
Spoon this mixture into the cups, and serve 2 to each person.

PEAS AND POTATOES

An early summer tradition in the Midwest is to harvest the first "pinky" potatoes
from the garden and serve them along with peas. For more flavor, the peas can be
steamed with a few of their empty pods.

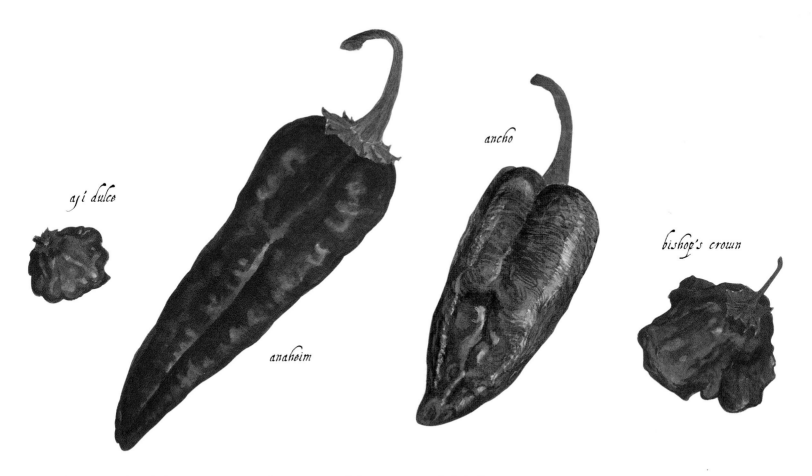

ayi dulce

anaheim

ancho

bishop's crown

These colorful, compact plants are like tropical birds that happened to alight in the garden. The number of open-pollinated sweet bell peppers offered in seed catalogs has fallen off markedly in recent years. But gardeners show new interest in sweet peppers of other shapes, and hot peppers are enjoying a boom. There's more to a hot pepper than heat, and gardeners find subtleties that are missing in a can of ground cayenne or a jar of pickled peppers.

PEPPERS

GROWING

Set seeds ¼ inch deep in flats about 8 weeks before you'll be planting outdoors. Use bottom heat to lift the medium's temperature to at least 75 degrees F. Once seedlings show true leaves, transplant them 3 inches apart in flats or in small pots; for sturdy plants, moderate temperatures to around 70 degrees F. by day and 60 at night. Provide plenty of light. In the garden, space peppers at least 12 inches apart, with no less than 2 feet between rows. A phosphorus-rich fertilizer will help these plants adapt and yield well.

Peppers can be grown easily in pots and placed on patios and decks or inside on sunny windowsills as houseplants.

HARVESTING

Pick peppers continually to encourage more fruits to set. The riper the pepper, the sweeter and more complex its flavor. A green pepper is an immature pepper, with a tart, rather thin taste—better than no pepper at all, and the best that gardeners with short seasons may be able to produce. But try allowing plants to enjoy the full stretch of the season for the sweetest, most-interesting fruits. A pepper's vitamin quotient goes up as it ripens as well.

The flavor of hot peppers becomes more complex with drying, adding overtones far from the garden, much as a wine can taste grassy or a Hebridean Scotch of vanilla. To air-dry peppers, choose varieties with thin walls (others are prone to spoiling). When thoroughly dried, peppers are best stored in an airtight container in a cool, dark place. Or you can tie their stems with string to make a long chain, or *ristra,* and hang them in full view.

You can also dry peppers in the oven at 200 degrees F. for six to eight hours. To make chili powder, grind dried chilies in a blender or food processor. Combine the powder with oil, vinegar, and crushed garlic to make chili paste.

Some peppers are traditionally dried over a fire. The products of this smoky ritual may be given another name: A Jalapeño becomes a Chipotle, a Chilaca becomes a Pasilla, a Poblano becomes an Ancho. Smoking can successfully process peppers with walls too thick for drying in the sun or an oven. In *The Pepper Garden* (Ten Speed Press, 1993), Dave DeWitt and Paul W. Bosland say that peppers can be smoked in a covered cooker, such as a Weber, as long as it is extremely clean—that is, not redolent of past meals. Build a conventional fire with charcoal briquets, and produce the fragrant smoke by adding water-soaked wood from nut or fruit trees such as oak, hickory, or apple. The low, smoldering fire may take a couple of days to dry a batch of peppers.

Before use, dried hot peppers are usually reconstituted by soaking in hot water for 15 minutes, or until softened and pliable.

SAVING SEEDS

Because seeds for many varieties are difficult to find commercially, pepper gardeners do a lot of seed saving and swapping. Peppers usually are self-pollinating, but to ensure that insects don't do any genetic experimentation of their own (hot pepper varieties are especially prone to cross-pollination), allow at least 50 feet between plants from which you will be taking seeds. To be really sure of keeping a strain pure, limit yourself to growing just one heirloom hot pepper in any one season.

Collect seeds when the fruits have reached the color of their maturity. Allow the seeds to dry on paper towels before storing. Another source of seeds is the dried peppers you buy for cooking. Tuck the seeds in a warm seed-starting medium and within a few months you may be harvesting the bright, fresh form of the mummified parents.

HOT

Ají Dulce. These cute little peppers are found in a variety of colors, from green through yellow and orange to red. *Dulce* means "sweet" in Spanish, but don't be misled into thinking you can nibble these peppers with impunity. They can be hot, although some gardeners report them to be surprisingly mild.

Anaheim. Anaheim has gone mainstream, appearing in supermarket produce departments around the continent, where its modest heat is not a threat to unwitting shoppers. There are sold both green and in the red, ripe form shown here. Anaheims are a common choice for *rellenos*, and can be cooked down into sauces. They will take on more personality if grilled.

Ancho. This variety, properly known as Ancho when dried and Poblano when fresh, can be made into

HOT PEPPERS, CAUTIOUSLY

Here are a couple of ways to gently introduce hot peppers to your cooking. As a first step in sautéing or stir-frying, scoot a pepper around the hot oil and then remove it before adding the other ingredients. Or tie a string to a hot pepper and dangle it in a sauce or soup only as long as its services are needed.

rellenos, salsas, and the sauces known as *pipians*. They are markedly sweet, fruity, and "quite hot but not painful," in the words of one seed saver.

Bishop's Crown. It looks like a hat that someone mistook for a seat cushion. Remove the seeds and membrane to moderate its heat.

Bulgarian Carrot. This curious heirloom from Bulgaria produces highly ornamental clusters of what appear to be shiny little carrots. The small plants can be grown in pots wherever mixed flower beds are looking a little thin and weary. The peppers have a fruity heat, and their color recommends them for salsas, chutneys, and marinades.

Cascabella. Little known several years ago, Cascabella is newly popular among gardeners. This moderately hot variety is suited to making sauces and drying. Shepherd's Garden Seeds suggests stuffing Cascabellas with cheese as a snack to serve with beer.

Chilhuacle Rojo. Gardeners who want a tamer pepper might like this friendly, approachable, easy-to-grow variety. The blistering heat may not be there, but the peppers take on notes of cherry and licorice when dried; the dried form of the related Chilhuacle Negro is also illustrated in this chapter. Seed savers brought these varieties north from Chiapas State in Mexico.

Chimayo. This New Mexico pepper's changing color is an indicator of its temperature—mild when green, and moderately hot when ripened to red. The peppers are used to make *ristras*.

Czechoslovakian Black. This is a mildly hot heirloom introduced recently from Europe. It has a short growing season and is easy to grow. With its unusual fruits and purple flowers, it makes a good ornamental for planting in pots.

De Árbol. Also known as Tree Chili, this pepper looks something like its relative the Cayenne, and like Cayenne it is often dried and powdered. The flavor is complex and quite hot.

Habanero. In their crayon-box colors, these little peppers look something like kids' toys, but behind the cheery appearance is the world's hottest gustatory experience. How hot? Chew on a piece of Jalapeño, multiply by 30, 40, or 50, and that's a Habanero. They aren't just pure burn, but offer a fruitiness— mango, papaya—to those who can handle them. Uses include salsa, marinade, and bottled sauce.

Hinkelhatz. In the midst of hot peppers with Latino names is this Pennsylvania Dutch specialty. The name means "chicken heart," for its appearance. It is available at present only through backyard seed savers. William Woys Weaver, whose specialty is Pennsylvania Dutch horticulture, says that this variety has been

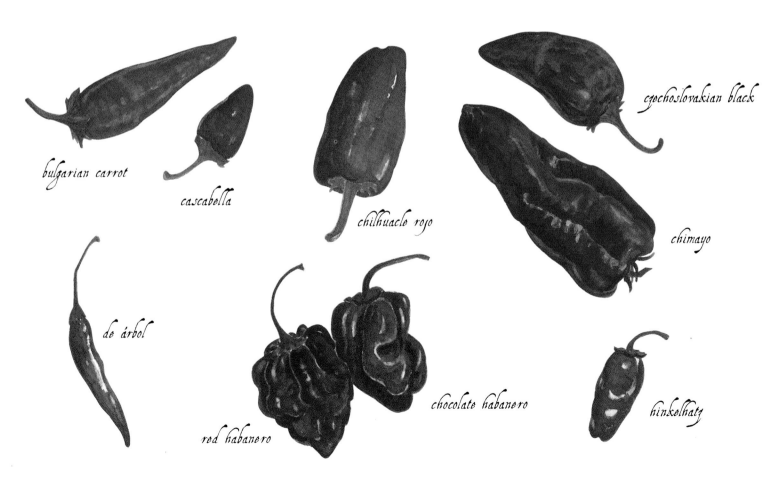

bulgarian carrot

cascabella

chilhuacle rojo

czechoslovakian black

chimayo

de árbol

red habanero

chocolate habanero

hinkelhatz

grown in the region for more than 150 years. Hinkelhatz are traditionally used to flavor pickled foods and vinegar.

Jamaican Hot. The Jamaican Hots are members of a fiery triumvirate that includes the Habaneros and Scotch Bonnets. They are used in all manner of Caribbean dishes.

McMahon's Texas Bird. An Army captain stationed in Texas sent seeds of this pepper to Thomas Jefferson at Monticello in 1812. Jefferson passed on seeds to a Philadelphia nurseryman whose name stuck to the pepper. Monticello continues to make the variety available to gardeners. The dwarf plants can be grown in pots and placed about the property for ornament.

Scotch Bonnet. This pepper looks something like a Habanero and is nearly as hot. Its smoky flavor finds

its way into Caribbean curries. Rhode Island pepper gardener Phil Hoffman names this one as his favorite of the one hundred fifty varieties he grows.

Serrano. They're shaped like bullets or flames—a reminder that the heat of a Serrano can startle the uninitiated. The green form is shown here; you may find both it and the sweeter red, ripe pepper offered by grocers. Serranos are often pickled.

Thai Orange. The Thais are hot and beautiful, make good houseplants in a sunny window, and are an authentic way to add heat to Thai dishes.

Yellow Squash. This squat pepper is also called Yellow Mushroom for its shape. A red form is available as well.

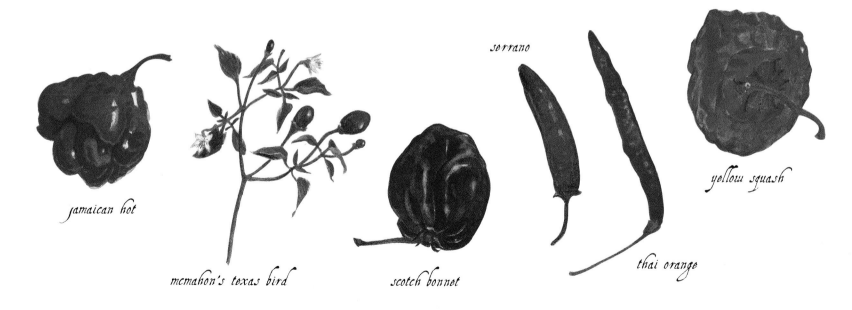

jamaican hot

mcmahon's texas bird

scotch bonnet

serrano

thai orange

yellow squash

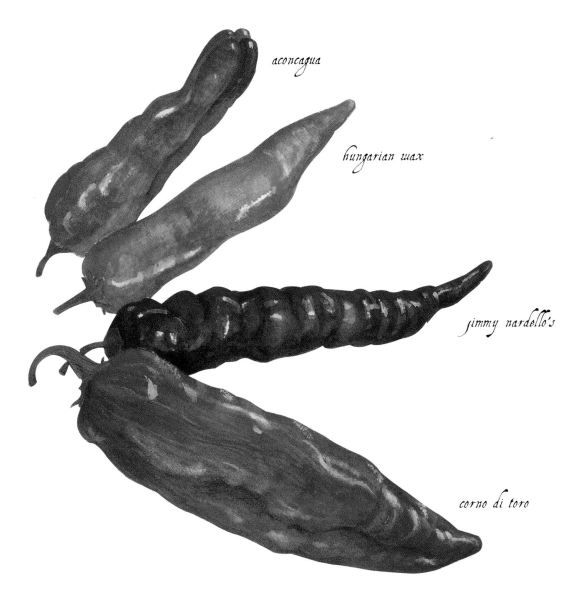

aconcagua

hungarian wax

jimmy nardello's

corno di toro

SWEET

Aconcagua. Unlike familiar bell peppers, this Argentine variety is sweet when still green. Aconcaguas can be used raw in salads, or try them fried or roasted.

Corno di Toro. The name, from its native Italy, means bull's horn, and the fruits do grow into long, sharply pointed shapes. The flavor is mild but not without character. Use them in salads or grill or sauté

them to bring out their character. The yellow variety is shown here in the process of ripening; you can also buy a lipstick-red cultivar. Plants are robust and very productive, and will be a standout in the garden. Note that hybrid versions of both yellow and red Corno di Toros are also on the market.

Hungarian Wax. You can find this common long pepper in both seed catalogs and the supermarket. The mild flavor improves with frying. Hungarian Wax is in

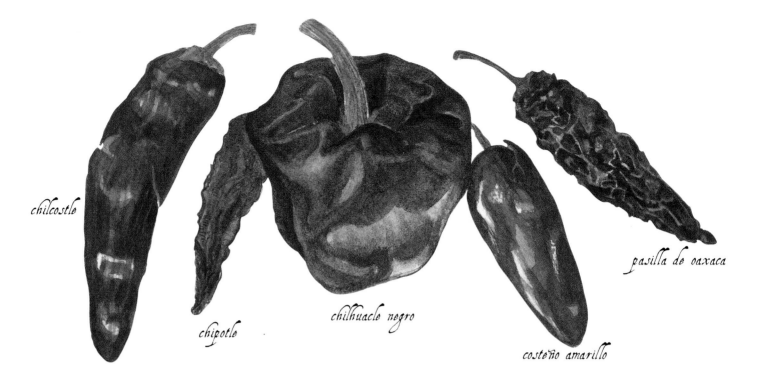

chilcostle

chipotle

chilhuacle negro

costeño amarillo

pasilla de oaxaca

fact a group of closely related peppers, also listed as Hungarian Banana among other names.

Jimmy Nardello's. Seed Savers Exchange has made this Italian heirloom frying pepper available to gardeners. Its flavor is distinguished by hints of spice and smoke. Preserve by freezing or drying.

DRIED

Chilcostle. The Chilcostle offers moderate heat and flavors of citrus and spice. Traditional uses include *mole* sauces and soups.

Chilhuacle Negro. This variety looks something like a bell pepper, starting off green and then maturing to a chocolate color. It is only mildly hot, and has a dark, tobacco-like character with a suggestion of licorice. It originated in Oaxaca, Mexico.

Chipotle. A Chipotle is a smoked, dry Jalapeño. It registers in the middle of the heat scale, and nuances include chocolate and tobacco. Chipotles are used in soup and salsas.

Costeño Amarillo. Mark Miller, pepper expert and author of *The Great Chili Book* (Ten Speed Press, 1991), can identify a range of nuances in this little dried variety—lemony citrus, green tomato, grass. It is modestly hot and traditionally finds use in yellow *mole* sauces and soups.

Pasilla de Oaxaca. Tobacco, smoke, and considerable heat come off this dried pepper from the Mexican state of Oaxaca. Its principal use is for *rellenos*. The fresh peppers are brownish black when fully ripened. Their heat is concentrated in the veins and seeds, and the flesh itself is quite mild.

CHIPOTLE POLENTA

*Here's a way to ease into using hot chili peppers. The recipe calls for just
enough of them to contribute a little heat to the dish. A Chipotle is a smoked, dried
Jalapeño, available through mail order (see page 185); you can also grow
and prepare your own. There is no need to buy an expensive packaged polenta
mix; just use coarsely ground cornmeal. This recipe isn't very involved,
but note you'll need preparation time: 15 minutes to soak the Chipotles and
at least an hour to refrigerate the polenta until firm.*

2 Chipotles

1 cup boiling water

15 Purple de Milpa tomatillos
   or 2 dried peach halves
   or 4 dried apricot halves

1 ripe bell pepper

2 teaspoons salt

2 cups yellow cornmeal

½ cup shredded jack or mild
   cheddar cheese

Olive oil

Put the Chipotles in a small bowl, pour the boiling water over them, and let soak
for 15 minutes. Using a very sharp knife or scissors, cut the Chipotles into fine
threads. Chop the tomatillos and the bell pepper. Put 6 cups water on to boil in a
large pot. Heat a skillet, add 1 tablespoon of olive oil, and sauté the Chipotles,
tomatillos, and bell pepper for 5 minutes. With the water at a low boil, add to it the
sautéed ingredients and the salt. Slowly stir in the cornmeal, using a whisk and
making sure that clumps do not form. Use a spoon to stir in the grated cheese.
Continue to stir occasionally for 10 minutes as the mixture thickens and becomes
somewhat gelatinous.

    Lightly oil a 9-x-13-inch baking dish. Pour and scrape the hot polenta into the
dish. Distribute in an even layer and all the way to the edges by pressing with the
back of a broad, sturdy spatula. Allow the polenta to cool somewhat, then refrigerate
until firm, at least 1 hour. Shortly before serving the polenta, cut it into squares and
brown lightly in an oiled pan, allowing about 5 minutes per side. Serve warm.

MRS. ADAMS'S PEPPER HASH

The author's great-grandmother, Edna Bloom Carter of Whitley County, Indiana, penciled this recipe on a blank page of a cookbook. The identity of the pepper-loving Mrs. Adams has been lost. This is a tarter version than hers, substituting a jot of molasses for three cups of white sugar. Serve the hash as a pasta topping, spoon it over baked potatoes, or use it as an omelet filling.

2 onions, chopped

8 red bell peppers, diced

1 hot pepper, finely minced
(optional)

3 tablespoons olive oil

¼ cup red wine vinegar

1 tablespoon molasses

2 teaspoons salt

Sauté the onions and the peppers in the olive oil in a large skillet until all are well softened, about 15 minutes. Mix the vinegar, molasses, and salt in a bowl and pour over the sautéed vegetables. Simmer, uncovered, for 15 minutes, stirring occasionally. Serve warm.

PASILLA ALMOND SAUCE

This recipe is adapted from one developed by the people at Native Seeds/SEARCH. Along with many chili pepper seeds from the Southwest and northern Mexico, they sell Pasilla powder and whole Pasillas. In this sauce, the pepper, almonds, raisins, and chocolate work together in a remarkable way. Use it over rice or as a dip with chips.

1 onion, chopped

3 cloves garlic, minced

2 tomatoes, chopped

2 tablespoons sesame seeds, toasted

½ cup almonds, toasted

¼ cup raisins

3 tablespoons olive oil

¼ teaspoon ground coriander

¼ teaspoon ground cloves

¼ teaspoon ground cinnamon

2 tablespoons Pasilla powder

1 tablespoon cornmeal

1 to 2 ounces bitter chocolate,
slivered

Salt

Puree the onion, garlic, tomatoes, sesame seeds, almonds, and raisins with ½ cup water in a blender or food processor until smooth. Heat the oil in a large saucepan and stir in the coriander, cloves, cinnamon, Pasilla powder, and cornmeal. Pour in the puree from the blender, ½ cup water, and the chocolate. Simmer for 10 minutes, stirring occasionally. Add salt to taste. Serve warm.

BOONE'S CAROLINA
ROASTED HOT PEPPER SAUCE

MAKES 1 QUART

At the end of every summer, R. Boone of Boone's Native Seed Co. makes up several batches of pepper sauce, complete with labels, for distribution to friends. This is an adaptation of his recipe.

You will have to begin by making Habanero powder from some fresh chilies. Spread the chili peppers on racks or baking sheets in the oven and roast them at 180 to 200 degrees F. (the warm setting) for four to six hours, or until they are brown and crisp. Turn occasionally if you are using baking sheets. Remove the stems and grind the peppers in a blender until powdered.

1 onion, finely chopped
4 cloves garlic, minced
1 tablespoon olive oil
1 tablespoon salt
¾ cup hot water

1 tablespoon roasted Habanero powder
2 teaspoons cayenne
Apple cider vinegar

Sauté the onion and garlic in the oil, then stir in the salt and hot water. Put the Habanero powder and the cayenne in a 1-quart bottle and fill halfway with the vinegar. Add the onion mixture, top off with vinegar, and seal.

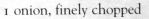

 *Peppers are also used in Grilled Vegetable Lasagna (page 77).*

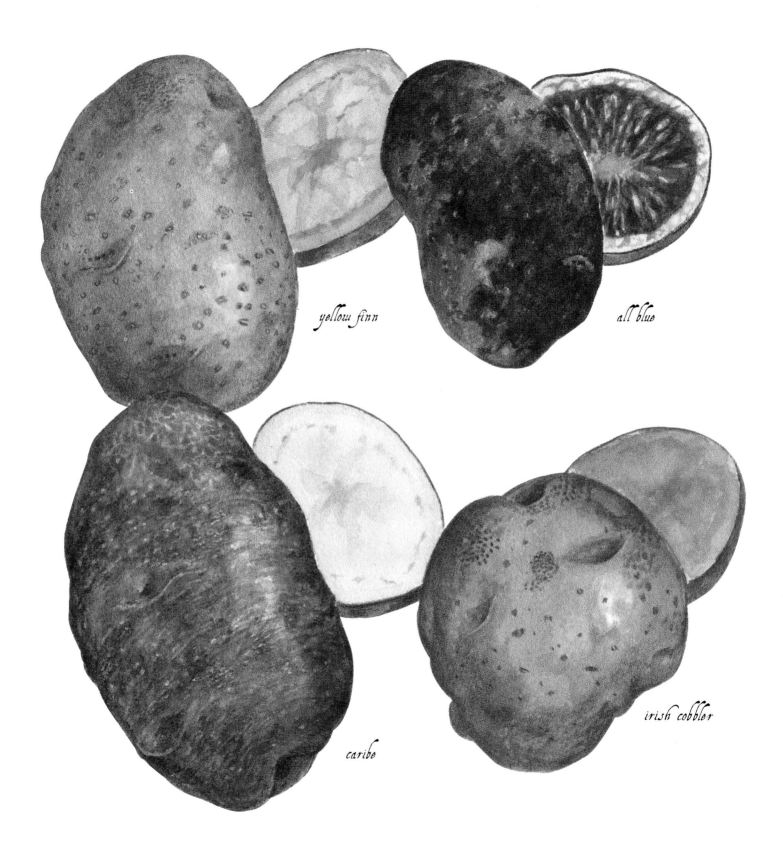

yellow finn

all blue

caribe

irish cobbler

As a working-class vegetable, the potato has only recently come to the attention of innovative chefs and gardeners looking for something new to try. Many of us had been lulled into thinking of potatoes as generic lumps of starch, redeemed by being dropped into a fryer or topped with fatty trimmings. Now seed catalogs have responded to the

POTATOES

potato boom by offering hundreds of varieties that not long ago had been unavailable commercially. And, remarkably, yellow and blue potatoes are winking out at us from supermarket produce bins.

Potatoes are often classified by size and shape. Fingerlings are small and longer than round, as the name suggests. Big, round, "potato-shaped" varieties are known as bakers or boilers. Texture is another quality used to describe potatoes. The word "waxy" is applied to varieties with flesh that is relatively moist and low in starch. These are suited for potato salads and sautéing—any type of preparation for which the potatoes should keep their shape. For baking, large and relatively dry potatoes are best because they will become properly flaky with cooking.

August Schuman, a Nebraska gardener who grows thirty or so heirloom potatoes, likes to combine yellow, red, and purple varieties in potato salads with color-coordinated ingredients—yellow spuds with yellow mustard and gray shallots, set off with a sprinkling of paprika, for example. He notes that the flesh keeps its color better if steamed rather than boiled. And, in an odd quirk of kitchen alchemy, you may find that hues become somewhat brighter with refrigeration.

GROWING

First decide on where the potatoes are to go. They shouldn't be grown in soil that has hosted potatoes or other nightshade family members (tomatoes, peppers, eggplant) in the past two to five years; the longer the period, the safer they'll be from disease. If that bit of advice leaves you feeling cramped for space, consider turning an annual bed into this year's potato patch. Potatoes aren't at all unsightly, just undramatic. And the All Blue variety offers pretty (if understated) blue flowers.

Potatoes are rarely grown from seed, but from what are confusingly known as seed potatoes—smallish tubers, the eyes of which will sprout new plants. These little potatoes can be tucked into the ground whole if very small; larger tubers are cut up into several pieces, each with at least one eye, to make several plants. If you will be dividing seed potatoes, try to do so a week before planting so that the cut surfaces have time to heal over as a means of preventing rot.

Order seed potatoes in early to mid-spring. Set them 3 to 4 inches deep and 1 foot apart with the eyes looking up, allowing 3 feet between rows. When the plants are 6 inches tall or so, hill up the soil around the base or apply mulch; this prevents sunlight from turning exposed potatoes green and toxic.

HARVESTING

You may want to mark the calendar eight weeks after planting for an early harvest of new potatoes. A couple of these young walnut-size tubers can be taken from each plant by reaching into the soil and feeling around.

Get out the garden fork when the tops die down. The plants' work is done, meaning the potatoes are ready to be exhumed. This is fun, as garden tasks go—a messy version of an Easter egg hunt—and a good job for children. Allow the potatoes to dry out of direct sunlight, then brush the dirt from them and store in a cool, dark place. Any potatoes that have become green from exposure to light are inedible and should be discarded (or used for seed potatoes the following year).

SAVING SEED POTATOES

For next year's crop, set aside smallish tubers from vigorous, healthy plants. Store them in a dark place, just a bit above freezing when possible.

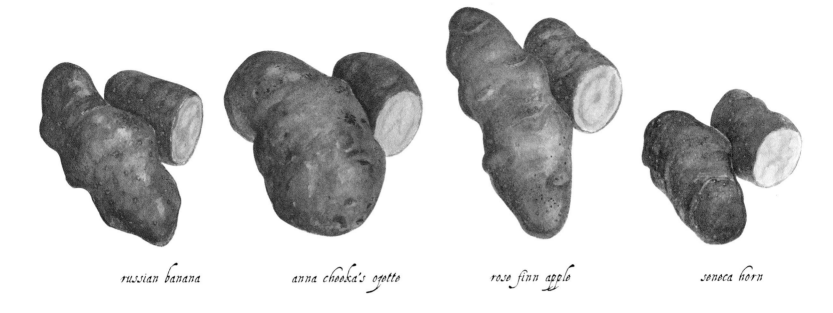

russian banana   *anna cheeka's ozette*   *rose finn apple*   *seneca horn*

VARIETIES

All Blue. With cooking, this productive Peruvian fades attractively and becomes fluffy. The earthy, nutty flavor suggests All Blue is high in minerals drawn from the soil. It yields plentifully and is a good keeper.

Anna Cheeka's Ozette. The story goes that the Spanish encountered this variety in the late 1700s while visiting the Makah-Ozette nation in the potato-blessed Andes. The flavor is mellow and squashlike.

Caribe. Despite the exotic-sounding name, this potato hails from New England. It is highly regarded for making mashed potatoes, and yields generously.

Irish Cobbler. Folklore has it that the name refers to an immigrant shoemaker in New Jersey who selected the variety from Early Rose potatoes. This is a good one for boiling or baking.

Rose Finn Apple. This is a particularly flavorful fingerling, with a waxy texture and yellowish flesh. It is thought that the variety originated in France.

Russian Banana. This potato migrated from the Baltic region to Canada, where it remains popular. It is a waxy, firm fingerling. Johnny's Selected Seeds suggests digging up smallish tubers in summer for potato salads. Another John—Dillinger—put a Russian Banana to clever use, whittling a pistol from it and breaking out of jail.

Seneca Horn. Seneca Horn is thought to have been developed by the Seneca Indians of New York State. The flavor is remarkably suggestive of butter, mayonnaise, even cheese.

Yellow Finn. The flesh is yellowish, the flavor mild and, to some tastes, buttery. Boil or bake this potato.

CHARCOAL-BAKED POTATOES

Potatoes can be baked over a charcoal fire for an extraordinary smoky flavor, tasting something like the roasted chestnuts bought from sidewalk stands.

Wrap larger potatoes individually in aluminum foil. Wrap fingerlings together in packets. Place on the grill when the coals have died down some and put the unit's cover in place if it has one. Baking times vary greatly; test to see if the potatoes are done by poking through the foil with a fork. To make the skins crisp and add flavor, open the foil packets for the final 10 minutes or so.

HIMMEL UND ERDE

SERVES 6

The name of this traditional German dish means Heaven and Earth,
but there is nothing world-shaking about its ingredients or preparation. Indeed, a
standard version involves adding homemade applesauce to mashed potatoes,
with butter and vinegar. This recipe, which calls for cooking the apples and potatoes
separately, allows each to maintain its identity in the blend.

6 cups peeled and cubed potatoes	1 teaspoon ground cardamom
6 firm apples, peeled and cubed	1 teaspoon salt
¼ cup olive oil	1 teaspoon ground black pepper
¼ cup wine vinegar	4 tablespoons butter (optional)

Steam the potatoes in a medium saucepan. Sauté the apples in 2 tablespoons olive oil in a large skillet. Cover both and cook until tender, stirring the apples as needed, about 10 minutes for the potatoes and 5 minutes for the apples. Drain the potatoes and add to the apples. Add the remaining 2 tablespoons oil, the vinegar, cardamom, salt, and pepper. Stir well, breaking up the cubes as you do so, and continue to cook for 5 to 10 minutes. If you will be using the butter, melt it in a small saucepan until just browned. Drizzle it over the pan of Himmel und Erde before serving.

Oven-Roasted Potatoes
with Rosemary

Lighter by far than french fries and more fun than baked potatoes, this method of preparation treats homegrown potatoes simply and gently. Use fingerlings or small potatoes of other varieties.

Preheat the oven to 400 degrees F. Cut potatoes into chunks no more than 1 inch in size. Combine olive oil, very finely chopped fresh rosemary leaves, and salt in a bowl and roll the potatoes around in the mixture. Place the potatoes in a baking dish and bake, turning from time to time, until tender and browned, about 40 minutes.

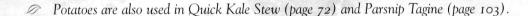

Potatoes are also used in Quick Kale Stew (page 72) and Parsnip Tagine (page 103).

Some gardeners go through a lifetime of growing seasons without planting a single radish seed, but for others this easily grown vegetable is the perfect bite-size, low-cal snack. Every month can be radish month. Spring and winter varieties are planted early and late in the season. Mid-season radishes handle the heat of summer without turning unpleasantly hot themselves. And shallow-

RADISHES

rooted varieties can be sown in pots as houseplants for a winter harvest. Chances are you either care for radishes or you don't, and midlife radish converts seem to be nonexistent. So instead of singing this crop's praises, we'll go straight to the horticulture.

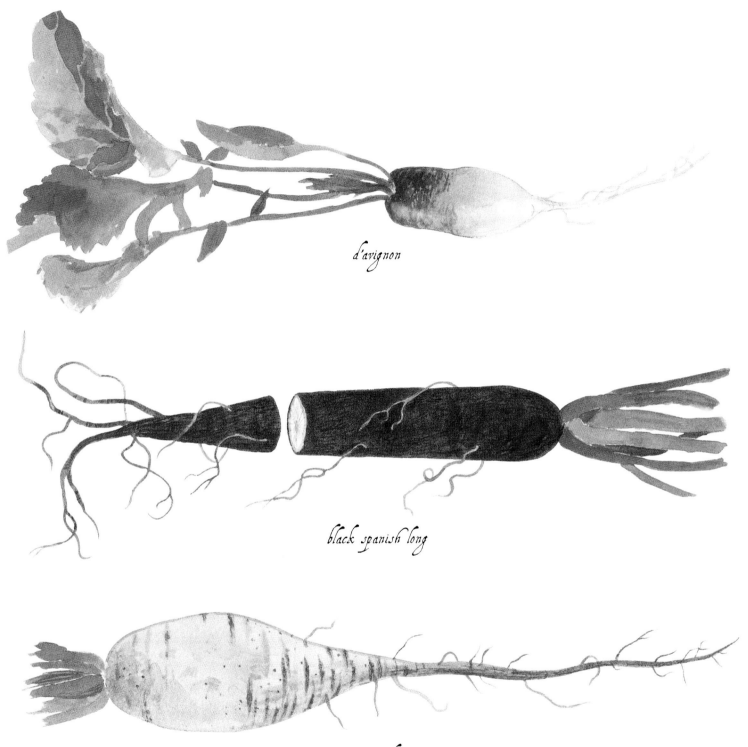

d'avignon

black spanish long

munich beer

GROWING

You can plant seed in the same row with carrots or other vegetables; the radishes will be ready to be pulled as their neighbors are under way. Set seeds ¼ to ½ inch deep, and ½ to 1 inch apart. Thin to 2 inches apart for all but winter radishes, which need twice the elbow room. For centuries, gardeners have anxiously watered radishes in hot, dry weather so that the roots won't respond by producing their own heat. Fearing Burr, Jr., suggested in 1865 that early radishes can be planted in the shade of asparagus ferns.

HARVESTING

Gather radishes as soon as the roots have matured in order to avoid cracking, toughness, and a harsh flavor. Keep them at their best by refrigerating in sealed plastic bags.

SAVING SEEDS

Radishes sown early in the season will produce seed heads that summer. Gather the yellowed seedpods, and bring them indoors to dry. Winter radishes are stored over winter, planted out the next spring, and allowed to complete their growth cycle.

VARIETIES

Black Spanish Long. The dark brown skin is in striking contrast to the firm, white flesh. The flavor is quite pungent, suggesting that people preferred a more assertive radish when this variety was developed, prior to 1828. Sow from late July to mid-August for a fall harvest. Black Spanish keeps well.

D'Avignon. These attractive, slender radishes are a traditional favorite from southern France. They need just three weeks until harvest, and should be pulled promptly to avoid pithiness.

Munich Beer. The large, tapering roots are a traditional accompaniment to beer in Bavarian beer halls. Sow seeds in midsummer for a fall harvest. Allow a few plants to go to seed and sample the edible pods.

Russian Radish Canapé

*Serve this pungent spread on thin slices of pumpernickel bread,
or place dollops of it on top of beds of salad greens.*

3 cups grated radishes	2 tablespoons wine vinegar
2 tablespoons sour cream	2 tablespoons chopped fresh dill
2 tablespoons plain yogurt	½ teaspoon salt

Grate the radishes. Combine well with the other ingredients in a bowl. Serve as a spread or salad.

Radish Hors D'Oeuvre

Radishes make a fine appetizer, best served with malty beer. Both the French and the British have traditionally dipped them in whipped butter; the bite of the vegetable is moderated by dairy products with some butterfat left in them. You might also try whipped cream to which white wine vinegar and salt have been added. Grated radishes go well with cream cheese in a sandwich. And rather than compost radish tops, combine them with other greens, chop finely, sauté until wilted, and remove from the pan. Heat a topping of sour cream, yogurt, and salt in the pan, and spoon over the greens.

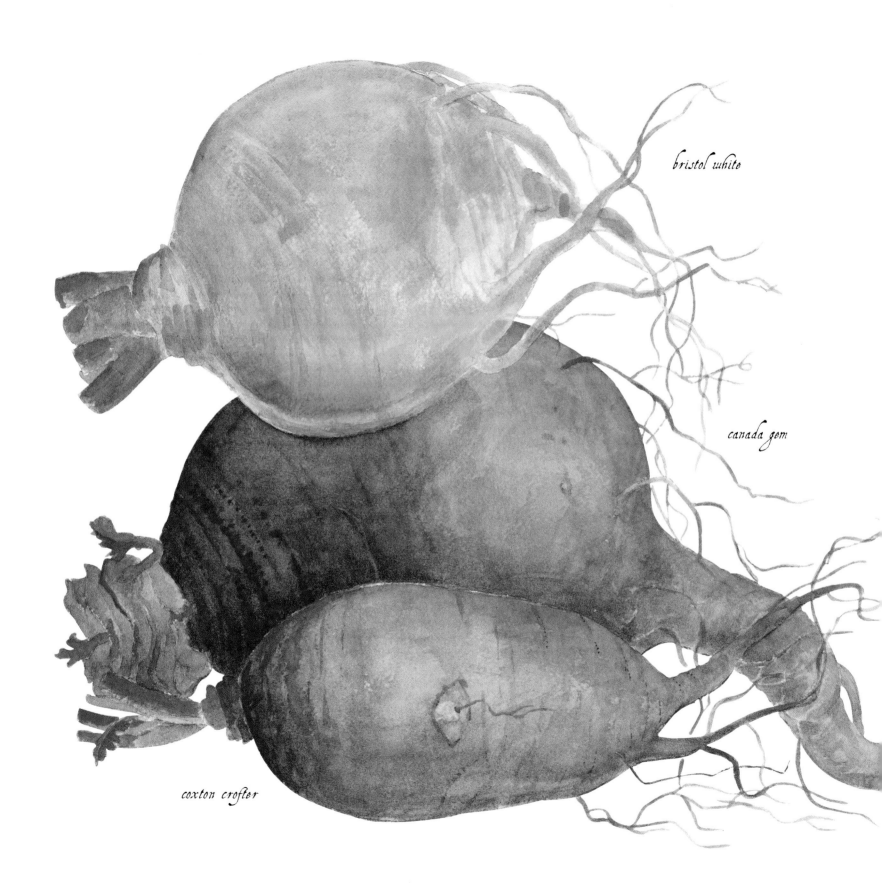

bristol white

canada gem

coxton crofter

The rutabaga needs to be rehabilitated. It is associated with serfdom and animal fodder, and an old edition of *Joy of Cooking* included just one rutabaga recipe—the same number granted to raccoon. Part of the rutabaga's image problem is its presentation in the supermarket—embalmed in thick wax. Checkout clerks are apt to look alarmed when this item rolls up the conveyor belt. And yet they are hardly anything new. Our

RUTABAGA

standard supermarket rutabaga, American Purple-Top Yellow, is the improved strain of a variety Fearing Burr, Jr., considered "old and long-cultivated" a century and a half ago. Most of the three dozen varieties offered through Seed Savers Exchange are listed by one man, Will Bonsall of the Scatterseed Project in Farmington, Maine. He provided two of the rutabagas shown here, Canada Gem and Coxton Crofter—varieties so rare that he asked they be mailed back once their portraits were painted. Although Will agrees that if you've seen one rutabaga, you feel as though you've seen them all, he does find interesting variations in this underappreciated vegetable.

Rutabaga also has an identity problem. Abroad, they are usually known as swedes, or Swedish turnips. Further confusing matters, rutabagas are usually distinguished from turnips by their yellow root, but some varieties are white fleshed.

GROWING

Plant as for turnips, but time the sowing about three months before the fall's anticipated first frost. Thin seedlings to a spacing of 7 inches. Rutabagas grow more slowly than turnips.

HARVESTING

Roots should be between 4 and 6 inches in diameter. Rutabagas will taste sweeter if they weather a couple of good frosts; in fact, crops grown in mountainous areas are said to be superior to flatland roots. When harvesting them, leave an inch or so of the tops on for increased storage life. You can keep rutabagas for up to half a year in a cool, damp place.

VARIETIES

Bristol White. This is one of many English varieties that has yet to establish itself in North America.

Canada Gem. Will Bonsall collected this variety from an elderly man in Waldoboro, Maine, the town immortalized by the Waldoboro Green Neck turnip. At present there is just one commercial source in North America. The flesh is sweet, fine grained, and pale yellow.

Coxton Crofter. This variety comes from Scotland, where rutabagas are a traditional accompaniment to haggis. The purple shoulders are typical. A crofter, by the way, is a Scottish tenant farmer, particularly of the Scottish Highlands and islands.

CHANCE ENCOUNTER

The rutabaga is thought to have come about as the chance cross between a turnip and a cabbage in medieval times. Its culinary reputation hasn't been promoted by its use as cattle fodder, or its role as a traditional accompaniment to haggis, the Scottish dish made by boiling a stomach stuffed with the minced heart, lungs, and liver of a sheep. To get acquainted with rutabaga, cut it into small cubes, steam until tender, and serve hot with butter and salt.

MASHED RUTABAGAS AND POTATO

SERVES 6

*To moderate the earthy bite of rutabagas (or enliven the subtlety
of potatoes), mash the two together. This symbiosis has been practiced
by Midwestern farmhouse cooks for many decades.*

4 medium potatoes, peeled and quartered ⅓ cup milk
2 rutabagas, peeled and diced ½ teaspoon salt
2 tablespoons butter ¼ teaspoon grated nutmeg

Steam the potatoes and rutabagas until tender, about 15 minutes. Mash them by
hand or with a blender or food processor, adding the other ingredients as you go.
Serve hot. Reheat if necessary.

jarrahdale

golden hubbard

green warted hubbard

The squashes include a small gang of different species, *Cucurbita maxima, C. mixta, C. moschata,* and *C. pepo*. Among them, the four represent dozens of varieties with a fascinating range of shapes, sizes, colors, and aptitudes. Some varieties are best enjoyed young, when the skin is still tender. These are termed summer squashes. Winter squashes are allowed to develop a durable skin, and often can be stored at cool room temperatures for months. In spite of these labels, you can eat a winter squash months early, as a summer squash, and live—in fact, you'll probably enjoy it.

SQUASH AND PUMPKIN

And what is a pumpkin? This isn't a genetically distinct plant, but merely a winter squash that happens to have a characteristic shape (roundish and ribbed) and color (orange, but sometimes white or blue).

North American heirloom gardeners are intrigued by squashes and pumpkins. The summer types are famously easy to grow. And the winter squashes are monumental, looking like beached creatures in the ruins of a frost-withered garden. Their brilliant colors hum visually like maple leaves but last right into winter as if they embodied sunlight. Bring a pumpkin indoors, and you have a cheerful reminder of when the days were longer and you were working up an honest sweat under the sun's high and commanding arc. The winter doldrums known as Seasonal Affective Disorder are treated with full-spectrum lighting, and it's tempting to think that pumpkin gazing might have a similar benefit.

Finally, squashes and pumpkins are special to us because we are mindful of these crops' associations with people and things profoundly American—Native Americans, for whom squashes were a vital food; the Colonists and their precarious fall harvests; and Halloween, now second only to Christmas in generating retail sales.

GROWING

Where should you lay out the squash patch? Project ahead a couple of months to a time when the bare ground will have become a sea of elephant-ear foliage and fat, raspy stalks. This will not be a welcoming Eden for someone clad in shorts and garden clogs. Try to find an out-of-the-way spot for these plants, so that they can sprawl and not get into too much trouble. Consider training squashes up a heavy-duty trellis or fence. A chorus line of winter squashes hanging from a white picket fence is a pleasing sight. As you set seed, remember to label your work with extra-large markers; standard-issue plastic plant tags will soon disappear under the plants they were supposed to identify.

Soak seeds for a few hours before planting. Sow them ¾ to 1 inch deep. Use 6 seeds to a hill for bushy plants, with hills spaced 3 to 6 feet apart; vining varieties need a minimum of 6 feet between hills. If you're planting in rows, bush varieties are spaced every 2 to 3 feet in rows 4 to 6 feet apart; vining varieties should be spaced every 3 to 4 feet in rows 8 to 12 feet apart. Ensure a good supply of water through the season. Slip straw, newspapers, or boards under squashes that are reclining on bare earth to keep them from rotting.

HARVESTING

The first squash harvest in many gardens is the over-size yellow blossoms. Native Americans have been putting them to use for centuries. They would stew blossoms along with baby squashes and enough cornmeal to make a thicker consistency. Snip the male blossoms, either as buds or just as they are about to open; they are larger than the females and lack the bulge of the developing fruit at the base. You won't reduce the yield by taking them, as long as you leave several to provide pollen. If you do use females, remove the pistil from the center. Store blossoms in a plastic bag in the refrigerator.

Pick summer squashes before they mature, or they're apt to be seedy, bland, and tough skinned.

To tell if a winter squash is ready for harvest, rap on it with your knuckles. If it's hard, it should be ready. Don't let winter squash sit out through the first hard frost, or storage life may be compromised. Leave a couple of inches of stem on the squash to discourage rot organisms from entering; the stem also will provide a convenient handle when it comes time to saw or hack open hard-skinned squash. It is a tradition to allow winter squash to cure—that is, develop a harder shell—either in the sun or in a warm room, for several days. For long-term storage, lug the squash to a dry spot where the temperature ranges in the 40s and 50s. Make sure that air can freely circulate around them.

SAVING SEEDS

Squashes like to mingle. They will cross-pollinate within their own species and may not breed true. That makes them ideal backyard genetics laboratories for gardeners who want to try creating their own varieties.

If you want to keep a strain pure, the easiest method is to plant just one variety from each species in any year. Or make sure that you are the only pollinator.

To do so, begin by placing bags over an equal number of budding male and female flowers just as they are about to open; female flowers are those with a swelling at the base. The following day, cut the bagged males from the plants. Open a female flower and, using tweezers, remove each stamen from the male flower and rub it against the stigma at the end of the pistil of the female flower you've just opened. Put the bags back over the females for at least three or four days to keep pollinating insects from spoiling your work. At harvest time, scoop out the pulp and seeds into a sieve, separate them under running water, and dry the seeds on a paper towel before storing them for the next season.

CUCURBITA MAXIMA

Blue Hubbard. Johnny's Selected Seeds mentions in its catalog that Blue Hubbard is a tradition at the roadside stands of New England. The distinctive clay-blue shell contrasts with the mustard-yellow flesh. It's a chore to hack through a Hubbard, but the flavor is rich and substantial, dry and quite sweet. (Note that dry-fleshed winter varieties are generally best when baked alone and for general cooking, while those described as moist-fleshed tend to be better suited for making pies.) As with other Hubbards, this is a good winter keeper.

Buttercup. A happy accident, Buttercup was the result of an unplanned cross between Quality and Essex Hybrid, and developed by the North Dakota Agricultural Experiment Station in the 1920s. The richly yellow flesh is sweet and dry, and Buttercup stores well.

Golden Hubbard. In contrast to the familiar blue-tinted variety, this one is a glorious orange, with a green knob on the blossom end as a distinctive field mark. Golden Hubbard was introduced in 1898. It stores well.

Green Warted Hubbard. Green and warted may not sound like the traits of a cute squash, but this variety is an attractive package, tapered at both ends, marked with pale stripes, and offering dry, sweet flesh. A relatively small one is shown here.

Jarrahdale. Seeds for this gray pumpkin were dropped by the Australian company that was the only source, and backyard seed savers maintained it until commercial interest revived in North America. The

buttercup

rouge vif d'étampes

blue hubbard

hard, deep-orange flesh is recommended for baking or pies; it takes on a complex, rich, even meaty flavor and makes cutting through the hard rind worth the effort.

Rouge Vif d'Étampes. This beautiful, trim pumpkin takes its name from a French town just south of Paris. It has a minor folklore role as the pumpkin that served Cinderella as a coach. Heirloom expert William Woys Weaver says that Rouge Vif d'Étampes was originally used in nineteenth-century France for soup stock. The variety made it to North America in 1883, and today it is usually relegated to decoration. However, the yellow flesh is thick and custardlike and good for pies.

CUCURBITA MIXTA

Green-Striped Cushaw. This most popular of the cushaws dates back to the early 1800s. Its moist, pale yellow-orange flesh deepens in color when baked and develops a good, pumpkiny flavor with a smoother texture than the White variety. Cushaws are excellent baked or made into pies. The Green-Striped variety can reach 40 pounds, but doesn't often go much over 10 or 15.

White Jonathan Cushaw. The smooth, near-white skin shows faint green markings, and the fruits can grow to 20 or 30 pounds. The moist, cream-colored flesh is mild and slightly fibrous, with a taste somewhat like spaghetti squash.

white jonathan cushaw

green-striped cushaw

CUCURBITA MOSCHATA

Butternut. It may not be flashy, but Butternut is an autumn staple for sautéing, baking, and pies. You might think from seeing Butternuts at every roadside stand that they are a living piece of Colonial heritage; in fact the variety was introduced in 1944. No one was talking about beta-carotene back then, but Butternut's dry, orange flesh happens to be an excellent source of this nutrient.

Neck Pumpkin. This is Butternut's ancestor, a wry-necked pie pumpkin that also has dry, thick flesh.

Rampicante Zucchetta. The curious shape of this curved squash has earned it another name from its native Italy, Tromboncino. It should be nipped from the vine when no longer than 18 inches in order to preserve the flavor—sweet, with a suggestion of artichoke. Allow the vines to climb a fence, sawhorses, or a proper trellis and grow them where they can be admired by visitors to the garden.

CUCURBITA PEPO

Benning's Green Tint Scallop. Scout the squash patch often to catch these attractive, cool-green pattypan squashes at their tender best—harvest when just 2 to 4 inches in diameter. Serve by cutting into cubes, steaming, and splashing with oil and vinegar.

Black Zucchini. The bushy plants of this zuke continue to push out fruits over an extended period. Although catalogs tell you to harvest them small, Black

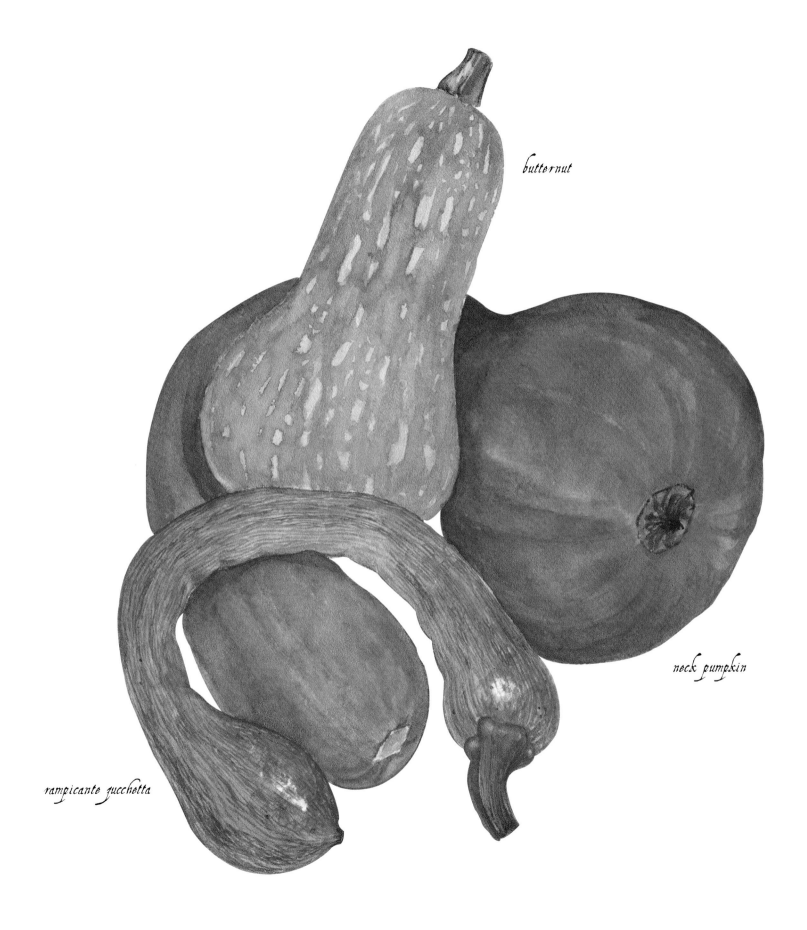

butternut

neck pumpkin

rampicante zucchetta

Zucchini remains tender and good as the fruits bulk up. Seed was first sold through the catalog of the Jerome B. Rice Seed Company in 1932.

Cocozelle. This relatively tidy zucchini grows as a bush. It originated in Italy as Cocozella di Napoli in the 1800s. The plants are highly productive, and the fruits are pleasantly firm with a somewhat nutty flavor.

Delicata. Delicata was introduced in 1894. As this winter squash matures, the colors warm and vivid orange patches may appear. Delicata's orangey yellow flesh is smooth and mild.

Ebony Acorn. This variation on the regular Acorn has a rounder shape and shallower ridges. It comes from the Arikara Tribe of North Dakota and had its commercial debut with the Iowa Seed Company in 1913. The plants are good producers. With its flavorful, nicely textured, pale orange flesh, Ebony Acorn is a traditional favorite for baking.

Ronde de Nice. In a garden full of tubular summer squash, this round French heirloom is a refreshing sight. The shape is pleasing, as is the light patterning. The plants grow as bushes, and the fruits quickly reach a harvestable size—pick them before they're more than 4 inches across for best texture and flavor. You can barbecue or even sauté these whole, if they're small enough. Or cut larger squashes in wedges, steam, and serve with oil and vinegar. If a few escape your notice and get big, stuff and bake them.

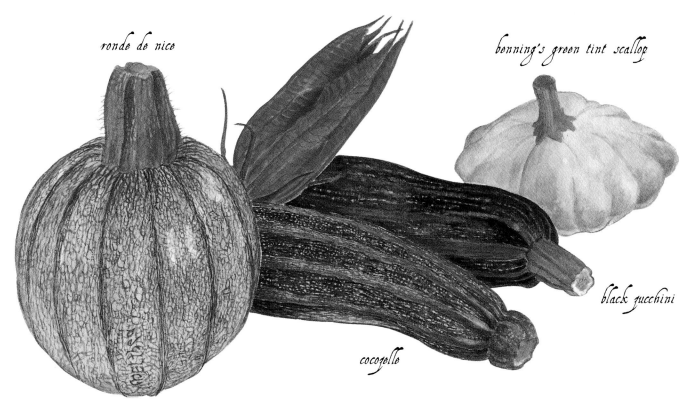

ronde de nice

benning's green tint scallop

black zucchini

cocozelle

small sugar

delicata

ebony acorn

winter luxury pie

turner's select

sweet dumpling

Small Sugar. Also known as New England Pie, this little gem predates the Civil War and has earned a reputation as perhaps the best all-round pumpkin. The flesh is fine grained and sweet.

Sweet Dumpling. As suggested by the name, this is a cute little winter squash with particularly sweet, interesting flesh—nutty and suggesting molasses and even turkey. Bake the halves with butter as you would Acorn. Dumplings can be stored into the winter without curing.

Turner's Select. Not often grown, Turner's Select goes through a few personality changes over the growing season. Try picking a few as summer squash, when small and green, and grill thick slices over charcoal with a garlicky marinade. Those left on the vine will gradually acquire interesting orange patterning, and develop in fall to orange, warted pumpkins. They are mild in flavor when baked.

Winter Luxury Pie. The name promises that this pumpkin will be something special, and some gardeners say Winter Luxury is the best pie pumpkin of them all. If you're put off by the prospect of having to cut through hard-shelled squashes, try this one—the skin isn't difficult to get through, and the orange flesh is moist and relatively soft. When cooked, Winter Luxury has a rich, almost oily texture and an unusual herbal scent.

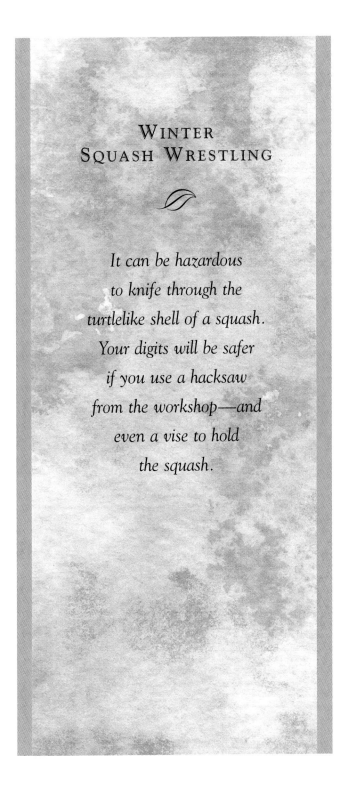

WINTER SQUASH WRESTLING

*It can be hazardous
to knife through the
turtlelike shell of a squash.
Your digits will be safer
if you use a hacksaw
from the workshop—and
even a vise to hold
the squash.*

SQUASH OR PUMPKIN PUREE

Bake or steam the squash or pumpkin, scoop the flesh from the shells, and reduce it to a creamy consistency in a blender or food processor. Preserve any surplus by freezing or canning.

BAKED OR STEAMED WINTER SQUASH

Winter squashes can be steamed, but their full flavor is brought out by the higher temperatures of sautéing and baking.

To bake squash, preheat the oven to 375 degrees F. Cut the squash in half and scoop out the seeds. Invert the halves, cut side down, in a baking dish with ½ inch water. (You can also bake smaller squash, such as Acorn, cut side up with a pat of butter in each hollow.) Check for doneness after 35 to 40 minutes; a larger squash may take more time. The cooked flesh of some varieties, Acorn among them, can be fluffed with a fork as you would spaghetti squash.

A more strenuous process is to peel the squash, cut it into 1-inch cubes, toss in a bowl with olive oil to coat, and bake for 20 minutes or so.

A third alternative is to place the whole squash in the oven and bake until tender, as indicated by lancing through the skin with a skewer. It will then be easy to cut through the softened shell.

To steam, cut the squash in half and scoop out the seeds. Add ½ inch water to a pan with a close fitting lid, and steam the squash cut side up until tender, replenishing the water as necessary. Or peel and cube them and cook in a steamer basket until tender.

HOT SUMMER SQUASH SALAD

The delicate flavor of summer squash can easily get lost in the shuffle of an involved recipe. This pared-down dish is quick to make and displays the color and flavor of the squash. Schedule the cooking so that the salad can be brought hot to the table.

4 small to medium yellow summer
   squashes
4 small to medium zucchini

1 tablespoon olive oil
1 tablespoon balsamic vinegar
½ teaspoon salt

Grate the vegetables and simmer with a little water in a nonstick skillet over medium-high heat, stirring and lifting so they don't become sodden or compressed. Combine the oil, vinegar, and salt in a serving bowl to make the dressing. When the squash is thoroughly heated but not limp, add it to the bowl, toss, and serve.

MARINATED ZUCCHINI

SERVES 4

The Podere le Rose cooking school in Tuscany guides its students through this unpretentious recipe.

1½ pounds small zucchini, cut into
   thin rounds
3 tablespoons olive oil
10 mint leaves, minced

3 cloves garlic, minced
4 tablespoons red wine vinegar
¼ teaspoon salt

Sauté the zucchini in the olive oil until lightly browned. Combine the remaining ingredients in a bowl to make a dressing. Place a layer of zucchini in a flat-bottomed bowl, spoon some of the dressing over, put down another layer, and spoon more dressing over. Continue layering until all the zucchini and dressing are used. Let sit at room temperature for at least 1 hour.

WINTER SQUASH SOUFFLÉ

SERVES 4 TO 6

*Squash lends its mild flavor, smooth texture, and warm color to a soufflé.
Use any winter squash or pumpkin from the garden. The recipe
is punched up with mustard, horseradish, and ground dried chilies,
but you should feel free to omit any of these.*

3 tablespoons butter

3 tablespoons unbleached all-
   purpose flour

1 tablespoon prepared mustard

2 tablespoons prepared horseradish

¼ teaspoon Pasilla or other chili
   powder

¼ teaspoon ground black pepper

¼ teaspoon salt

1¼ cups milk, scalded

¾ cup smoked mozzarella, shredded

¾ cup cheddar or jack cheese,
   shredded

2 cups squash puree, cooled (see
   page 146)

3 large eggs, separated

5 large egg whites

Preheat the oven to 375 degrees F. Oil an 8-inch soufflé dish.

Melt the butter in a saucepan and whisk in the flour, mustard, horseradish, chili powder, pepper, and salt. Stir in the milk. Switch to a wooden spoon and keep stirring for 10 minutes, or until smooth. Remove the pan from the heat and stir in the cheeses. Let cool, stirring occasionally.

When cooled, add the squash puree. Beat the egg yolks and whisk them into the squash mixture. Beat the whites until they form peaks. Fold into the squash mixture. Pour into the soufflé dish.

Bake for 35 to 40 minutes without opening the oven door (soufflés lose their loft if disturbed). Serve immediately.

PUMPKIN WHOOPIE PIES

*Farmers' markets and roadside stands throughout Pennsylvania
Dutch country sell these single-serving snacks. Chocolate and vanilla are standard
flavors, and pumpkin whoopies are a fall tradition.*

*A whoopie pie isn't a pie at all, but a pair of round cookie-size cakes,
bonded with a filling of frosting or cream. This version uses a whipped cream
filling; you can substitute a low-fat icing instead. The recipe calls
for half the sugar and oil found in most whoopies, and relies on applesauce
and oatmeal for sweetness and a good consistency.*

CAKE

- 3 egg whites
- 2 cups pumpkin puree
  (see page 146)
- ½ cup vegetable oil
- ¾ cup applesauce
- 1 teaspoon vanilla extract
- 1 tablespoon grated ginger
- ½ cup rolled oats
  (1-minute "quick" oatmeal)
- 1 cup (packed) brown sugar
- 3 cups unbleached all-purpose flour

- ½ teaspoon salt
- 2 teaspoons ground cinnamon
- ½ teaspoon grated nutmeg
- ½ teaspoon ground allspice
- 1¼ teaspoons baking powder
- 1¼ teaspoons baking soda

FILLING

- 1 cup heavy cream
- 3 tablespoons confectioners' sugar
- 1 teaspoon vanilla extract
- 2 teaspoons bourbon

Preheat the oven to 400 degrees F. Oil three baking sheets, 12 x 17 inches.

Beat the egg whites with a whisk until frothy, about 1 minute. Stir in the pumpkin puree, oil, applesauce, vanilla, ginger, and oatmeal. Allow the oatmeal to absorb liquid as you continue to work.

In another bowl, combine the brown sugar, flour, salt, spices, baking powder, and baking soda, using a whisk to mix thoroughly. Stir in the pumpkin mixture. Place spoonfuls of batter on the baking sheets. Distribute the batter evenly to make 30 or so whoopie halves, 3 inches in diameter. The cakes should be as round as you can form them. Leave space for them to expand while baking.

Bake for 10 minutes, or until the tops spring back when pressed with a finger. Remove from the oven and allow to cool *completely* to room temperature. If you are in a hurry, speed up this step by placing the halves in the freezer.

Meanwhile, whip the cream, adding the confectioners' sugar, vanilla, and bourbon, and continue to whip until the cream is stiff enough to form soft peaks.

Assemble the whoopies with the rounded sides out, spreading a layer of whipped cream between each pair. Serve immediately or wrap the pies individually and refrigerate for up to several hours.

ARKANSAS CUSHAW PUDDING

SERVES 6 TO 8

Arkansas gardener Tom Paetzel and his family like to use squash in a simple cornmeal pudding that might not be very far removed from an early Native American dish. Although Tom prefers White Jonathan Cushaws for the recipe, this version combines it with the richer, orangey Green Jonathan.

1 cup water	2 tablespoons vegetable oil
1 cup milk	¼ cup maple syrup
2 cups cornmeal	1 teaspoon ground cinnamon
1½ cups White Jonathan Cushaw puree (see page 146)	½ teaspoon grated nutmeg
	1 teaspoon salt
1½ cups Green-Striped Cushaw puree (see page 146)	Maple syrup, for serving
	Plain yogurt, for serving

Preheat the oven to 350 degrees F. Oil a 9-x-13-inch baking dish. Bring 1 cup water and the milk to boil over medium heat and slowly add the cornmeal, stirring constantly with a whisk so clumps do not form. Turn the heat down to low and simmer until the liquid is absorbed, about 10 minutes. Stir in the squash puree, oil, maple syrup, cinnamon, nutmeg, and salt, mixing well. Spoon into the baking dish.

Bake for 30 minutes. Serve warm with maple syrup and yogurt.

Pumpkin Pasta Sauce

SERVES 5 TO 6

*For a break from tomato-based pasta sauces, try this season's-end
alternative. It has the satisfying thickness and zest of a good red sauce,
made sensual with artichoke hearts and colorful with the vivid
ink of black currants (use any berries you may have in the freezer).*

4 tablespoons olive oil

1 medium onion, chopped

1 red bell pepper, chopped

2 cloves garlic, minced

8 to 10 fresh artichoke hearts,
  or 14-ounce can, chopped finely

2½ cups pumpkin puree
  (see page 146)

½ cup black currants
  (or other berries)

8 pitted olives

2 teaspoons garam masala, or your
  own combination of ground
  spices—cardamom, cinnamon,
  cumin, black pepper, cloves,
  and nutmeg

1 tablespoon brown sugar

2 tablespoons red vinegar

¼ cup pumpkin seeds

Hot cooked pasta, for serving

Put on water to cook the pasta. In a skillet over medium heat, add the oil and sauté
the onion and bell pepper for 2 or 3 minutes. Add the garlic and sauté for another
minute. Stir in the artichoke hearts, cook another minute, then follow with all of
the remaining ingredients except the pumpkin seeds. Cook for 10 to 15 minutes,
stirring occasionally. Toast the pumpkin seeds in a skillet or countertop toaster-oven.

To serve, spoon the sauce over each portion of pasta, and sprinkle pumpkin seeds
over the top.

Sweet potatoes aren't grown as often by gardeners as they might be because of an idiosyncrasy—they're started from slips, as the rooted sprouts are known. You may be able to find these perishable items sitting in a bucket of water at a local nursery; otherwise you'll

SWEET POTATOES

have to purchase roots through one of the few catalogs that bother with sweet potatoes or from other gardeners offering them by mail. Only one of the varieties illustrated here (Nancy Hall) is to be found in commercial catalogs, although all can be ordered through Seed Savers Exchange.

Northern gardeners tend to think of sweet potatoes as an obscurity they shouldn't get involved with, but some varieties have short seasons suited to cooler zones. And black plastic can be used to warm garden beds, from planting time right through summer.

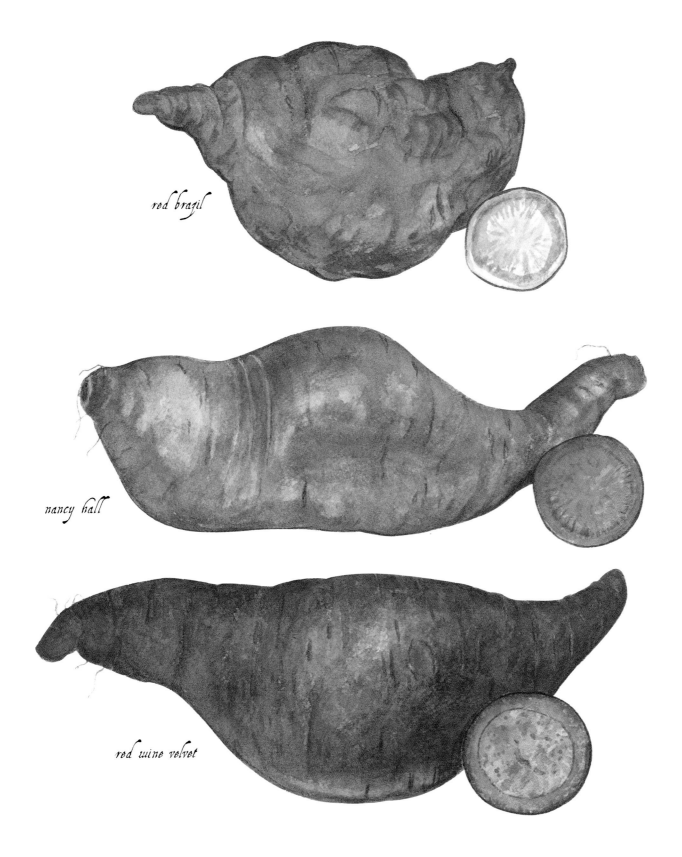

red brazil

nancy hall

red wine velvet

Another factor that might limit the sweet potato's popularity is confusion around just what this thing is. First of all, it is not a potato; the genus, *Ipomoea*, also includes morning glories, and in fact these vining plants do produce a similar flower. Nor is it a yam, a name mistakenly applied to yellow-fleshed sweet potato varieties.

A final blow is that sweet potatoes seem to attract marshmallows the way black sweaters do lint. They deserve better, and a couple of grown-up recipes are given at the end of this chapter.

GROWING

Because the harvestable part of the plant forms below ground, you should give extra thought to soil composition. Sweet potatoes do best in a sandy mix that's just on the acidic side.

The rooted slips are set out after the last frost is past and the weather has settled. Space them 12 to 15 inches apart in rows 3 to 4 feet apart, with the rooted half in the ground and the leaves just above the soil surface. You can give the roots a better chance of growing deeply by hilling up a ridge of soil, a foot or so high, and planting the slips in it.

HARVESTING

In the North, the signal that harvesttime has come is frost-blackened leaf tips; southern growers look for yellowed foliage. Sweet potatoes will be damaged by freezing, so dig them up promptly and cure for a couple of weeks in a warm, humid place where temperatures ideally hold above 80 degrees F. Leave a patina of soil on them; sweet potato growers warn that washing the roots will shorten storage life. Then wrap them in newspaper and store in a dark place with temperatures in the 50s—but not in the refrigerator.

STARTING SLIPS

Sweet potatoes don't grow predictably from seed. You'd find a great variation in the skin and flesh color, as well as shape. Some gardeners enjoy this gamble, and experimenting with seedlings has the same sort of serendipity as looking for shells along the beach. For predictable results, take slips from roots you're storing in the house. Begin to induce sprouting in early spring in cooler zones and in February in the South. Arrange each sweet potato in a jar of water so that water comes up an inch on it, as if starting an avocado from a pit. Or set them in a box of dampened sand, rotted sawdust, or potting medium, 2 inches or so below the surface. Keep the roots in a warm room, and within a few weeks you should see sprouts forming. When a sprout reaches about 6 inches, with clusters of both leaves and roots, the slip is ready and should be snapped off.

VARIETIES

Nancy Hall. This moist-fleshed, mild-flavored variety is suited for baking. It keeps well. Nancy Hall is available commercially, but sources have diminished over the past several years. Its popularity peaked more than a half-century ago.

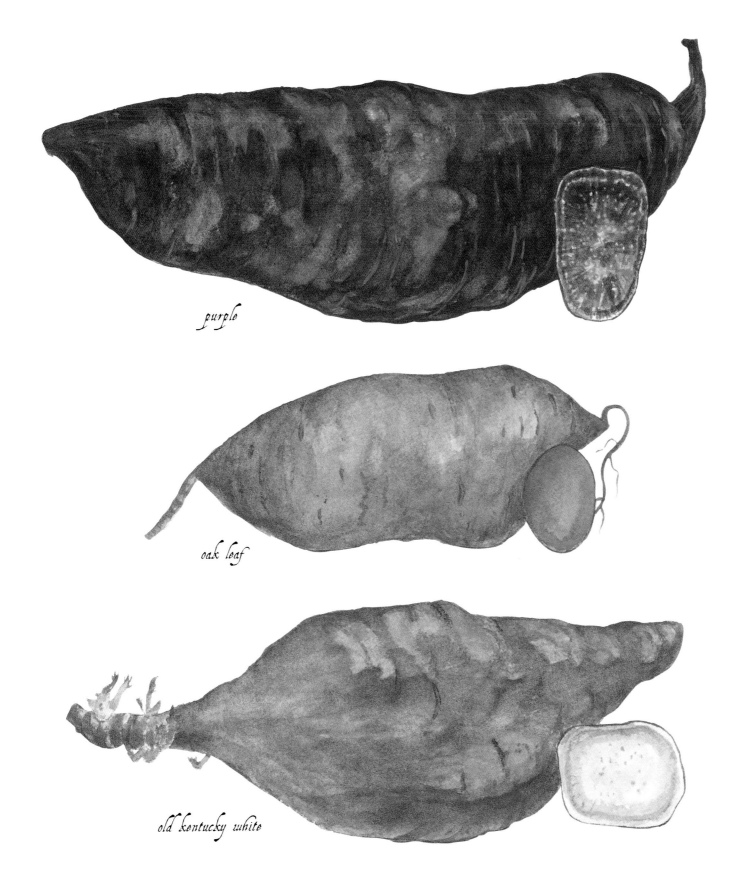

purple

oak leaf

old kentucky white

Oak Leaf. This obscure variety is distinguished above ground by the shape of its leaves. It yields a good crop of orange-fleshed roots.

Old Kentucky White. Although it has disappeared from catalogs, this sweet potato remains a popular item in Kentucky and southern Indiana. The cream-colored flesh is sweetly flavorful and without the stringiness found in some roots. David Phillips, the Indiana grower who supplied this sample, was given the variety by an elderly Kentucky woman whose family had grown it for more than fifty years. Old Kentucky is a good keeper and produces an ample supply of slips for the season ahead.

Purple. "I took some of these to a picnic," says sweet potato grower David Phillips, "and people kind of avoided them." But once the picnickers gathered their nerve and sampled the Purples, "they tied into them and cleaned the whole platter." This stunning variety can grow to 16 inches long.

Red Brazil. You expect a sweet potato to be sweet, but some fans of the vegetable prefer varieties that are less so. Red Brazil is an example. It was once commonly grown in Indiana and is now all but forgotten, according to Larime Wilson of the Wylie House Museum in Bloomington. The sample shown here is from the museum's collection, obtained from an elderly Vernon County couple.

Red Wine Velvet. That's a powerfully exotic name for a lumpy root. But this old-time variety combines purplish stems, wine-red skin, and moist, school-bus orange flesh.

GOLDEN KASHMIRI PILAF

SERVES 6

Pilafs are dishes found over an enormous geographical swath, along the Mediterranean and stretching across Asia. This version is from Kashmir, a predominately Muslim state in Northwestern India. Sweet and sour ingredients give the diced sweet potato in this recipe a caramelized coating. And the colors—yellow sweet potatoes, golden peppers, and carrots, burnished with turmeric and saffron—will make this dish glow even at a candlelit dining table. To turn the recipe into something more familiar, skip the rice and spoon the ingredients over pasta instead.

If you don't do much Indian cooking, you might want to check your supply of the spices listed here for freshness. Consider replacing any that have lost their potency.

1½ cups rice

1 onion, chopped

2 cloves garlic, minced

1 tablespoon vegetable oil

2 teaspoons grated ginger

1 teaspoon mustard seeds

2 teaspoons ground coriander

1 teaspoon ground cinnamon

1 teaspoon ground black pepper

½ teaspoon ground cardamom

½ teaspoon turmeric

½ teaspoon saffron

¼ teaspoon ground cloves

¼ teaspoon ground asafetida

1 teaspoon salt

3 tablespoons butter

2 tablespoons brown sugar

6 tablespoons lemon juice

2 sweet potatoes, cut into
    ¾-inch dice

1 yellow bell pepper, cut into strips

2 carrots, cut into thin coins

10 to 15 whole almonds, toasted

Bring 2½ cups water to a boil over high heat and add the rice. Reduce the heat and simmer until the water has been absorbed, about 25 minutes. Remove from the heat. Note that this is not enough water for the rice to cook fully; it continues to cook with the other ingredients.

Sauté the onion and garlic in the oil, then add the ginger, mustard seeds, coriander, cinnamon, black pepper, cardamom, turmeric, saffron, cloves, asafetida, and salt. Stir occasionally over medium heat for 2 or 3 minutes. Add the butter,

brown sugar, and lemon juice and stir. Add the sweet potatoes, bell pepper, and carrots and stir until all are coated with the spices. Add a few tablespoons of water as necessary to prevent scorching, cover, and continue to cook, stirring occasionally, for 10 minutes or until the vegetables appear to be about half cooked.

Add the rice to the vegetables and stir well to combine. Add water if needed, cover, and simmer for 10 minutes or until both the rice and vegetables are done. Crush the almonds with the back of a spoon and top each portion with some. Serve hot.

Sweet Potato Casserole

SERVES 5

Here is a way to transform the unsung sweet potato into a dish that tastes very much like cheesecake. The idea for the recipe comes from the people at Fred's Plant Farm in Martin, Tennessee, a company offering sixteen sweet potato varieties.

2½ to 3 cups cut-up (1-inch cubes)
  sweet potato
2 tablespoons butter
⅓ cup brown sugar
½ cup condensed milk
½ teaspoon nutmeg
½ teaspoon ground cinnamon
½ teaspoon vanilla extract
1 teaspoon salt
2 large eggs, beaten

TOPPING
2 tablespoons butter
2 tablespoons olive oil
½ cup toasted wheat germ
½ cup original-flavor Ovaltine
  or other malt powder

Preheat the oven to 425 degrees F. Oil a 9-x-13-inch baking dish.

Steam the sweet potatoes for 20 minutes, or until tender. Melt the butter in a saucepan, and stir in the brown sugar, condensed milk, nutmeg, cinnamon, vanilla, salt, and eggs. Place this mixture and the sweet potatoes in a food processor and reduce to a smooth batter. Spoon the batter into the baking dish.

To make the topping, melt the butter in a small saucepan, add the olive oil, and stir in the wheat germ and Ovaltine. Sprinkle the topping over the batter. Bake for 15 minutes. Serve warm.

toma verde

indian strain

purple de milpa

This South American annual is best known as the backbone of traditional salsa. But they deserve to be experimented with, especially the fruity, aromatic Purple de Milpa. Don't dismiss them as small,

TOMATILLOS

weird tomatoes—tomatillos are related, but their flavor is unique, with considerable variation among varieties. Tomatillos are easy to grow from seed, need little or no tending, and are very productive.

GROWING

The seeds sprout quickly and sprint to maturity. Start seeds as you would tomatoes. Set out the transplants 2 feet apart. Tomatillos tend to flop all over the place if left to their own devices. Plants can be tied up or grown in cages; or, more simply, keep soil hilled up around them.

HARVESTING

Fruits are enclosed in papery husks—hence the alternate name of husk tomato. Tomatillos can be picked in the green stage, but they are at their best ripe (especially if you won't be cooking them) when the husks are thin and papery and the fruits have changed color.

VARIETIES

Purple de Milpa. The sprawling plants yield smallish fruits that gradually turn a deep purple where the sun reaches them through the split husk. When ripe, they can be enjoyed raw. But they are exceptional when sautéed—the aroma, flavor, and mouthfeel (with all those tiny seeds) are remarkably close to those of warm raspberry pie. It's clear why this strain has been handed down through many generations.

Indian Strain. These tomatillos mature quickly and have a sweet-sour flavor, similar to apples, with a hard-to-define overtone of spice.

Toma Verde. Harvest when they have warmed from green to yellow. If you sauté Toma Verdes, they take on an almost cloyingly rich flavor—buttery, even meaty, and as sweet as if brown sugar had been stirred in.

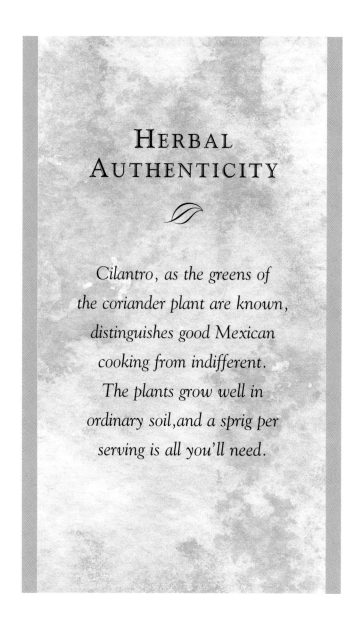

HERBAL AUTHENTICITY

Cilantro, as the greens of the coriander plant are known, distinguishes good Mexican cooking from indifferent. The plants grow well in ordinary soil, and a sprig per serving is all you'll need.

Purple de Milpa Blintzes

MAKES ABOUT 16 BLINTZES

*The bright, berrylike flavor of this variety cries out for a recipe that
allows it to shine, away from the heat and busyness of salsa.*

FILLING

3 cups quartered Purple de Milpa
  tomatillos

1 banana

1 teaspoon grated orange zest

¼ cup fresh orange juice

BATTER

1 large egg

2 large egg whites

¾ cup unbleached all-purpose flour

1½ cups skim milk

1 tablespoon butter

Butter, for frying

Sour cream, for serving (optional)

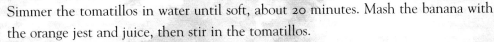

Simmer the tomatillos in water until soft, about 20 minutes. Mash the banana with
the orange jest and juice, then stir in the tomatillos.

Combine the batter ingredients in a blender and blend until smooth. Make 1
thin pancake at a time in a small, buttered nonstick pan, cooking one side only.
Remove each pancake, place about 1 tablespoon of filling across the middle, and roll
up. If you wish, spread a teaspoon of sour cream along the top of each blintz when
all are assembled. Serve warm.

BROILED SALSA AMARILLO

This yellow salsa is adapted from a recipe used by the people at Mapel Seeds in Massachusetts. The fruitiness of the tomatillos—Purple de Milpa in particular—combines with the smoky edge from broiling and the scent of lime. Use this fresh, piquant sauce with eggs, tortillas, grits, toasted cheese sandwiches, tofu, fish, chicken, and meat.

15 ripe tomatillos

15 Yellow Pear tomatoes or any variety of yellow cherry tomatoes

½ ripe Chilhuacle Rojo chili pepper, finely chopped; or ½ red bell pepper, finely chopped, plus ½ teaspoon hot pepper sauce

1 onion, finely chopped

1 clove garlic, minced

1 tablespoon olive oil

¼ cup minced cilantro

Juice of 1 lime

½ teaspoon salt

Cilantro leaves, for garnish

Quarter the tomatillos and tomatoes and broil them, either in a toaster oven or broiler, until their skins are darkened by the heat. Place them in a large bowl.

Sauté the chili pepper, onion, and garlic in the olive oil. Add them to the tomatoes and tomatillos. Add the cilantro, lime juice, and salt. Stir well, cover, and refrigerate for at least 4 hours to combine the flavors. Garnish with whole cilantro leaves.

✐ *Tomatillos are also used in Chipotle Polenta (page 117).*

costoluto genovese   *stupice*   *reisentraub*

It's a safe bet that most vegetable gardeners, if restricted to a tiny plot barely big enough to stand on, would choose to grow a tomato plant. Tomatoes are a treat for the senses, starting from the day they break through the ground. In their flats under the fluorescent glare, the tiny seedlings give off the first true scent of summer, winy, herbaceous, a little skunky—a preview of the sun-filled days to follow.

TOMATOES

Tomatoes are a treat for the eyes as well. Only the seeds, looking like flecks of cardboard, are without visual interest. Within days, the first true leaves appear, their deep notches suggestive of the tomato's subtropical origin. As the vines mature, their hairy stems take on an overtly defensive appearance. Then, with warm weather, the plants explode into green lavishness, turning into small, short-lived trees that stretch for the sun with a boarding-house reach. Yellow flowers appear like indicator lights, promising a bountiful harvest.

Then the fruits swell, sometimes to bursting. If you've planted a good selection of varieties, you have the treat of watching that well-known acid green change to any of a wide range of hues. There are warm and cool reds, yellows shading toward the orange of bittersweet, pastel pinks, and oddities in bruised purple, white—even something approaching black. The fruits of a few varieties don't change in color much at all but are harvested green.

Sizes vary from pea to limb-threatening jumbo. And traditional varieties come in all sorts of odd shapes and asymmetries, unlike the uniform roundness of supermarket tomatoes. At harvest, a tomato plant is as stunning as any bush in the suburban landscape. This recommends them in mixed beds as partners with perennials and larger annuals.

Then, more suddenly than seems possible, the season is over. The aggressive tomato plants become a blackened shambles. After their intense summer, it's as if the tomatoes' death is due to exhaustion rather than a change in the weather.

GROWING

Tomatoes are classified broadly as determinate or indeterminate, terms that refer to the plants and not the fruits. Indeterminate varieties sprawl all over the ground, taking up almost as much precious garden area as zucchini; and vines continue to grow and make blossoms and fruits until put out of commission at summer's end. We stake them and cage them to wrest some order.

In contrast, determinate varieties are moderate, tidy creatures. They grow to a point and stop. Because they take less space, determinates are a good choice for small plots and containers. An advantage for commercial growers is that the crop becomes ripe over a short period, making harvest simpler; but backyard gardeners who can't handle a glut of tomatoes may find this trait works against them.

Once upon a time, all tomatoes were indeterminate. Then, in 1914, the first determinate tomato appeared spontaneously, growing primly in a Florida field. Breeders pounced on it as a template for commercial varieties to come. Most heirloom varieties are indeterminate, however, and some tomato aficionados argue that indeterminates taste better. One theory is that they have more flavor-producing foliage per fruit than their modern competition.

Another bit of tomato lingo is "beefsteak," describing any variety with large (at least one pound) fruits that have meaty flesh, relatively few seeds, and little clear or transparent gel. "Potato-leafed" tomatoes sound like green Frankensteins, but they simply are varieties with foliage lacking the notches typical of tomatoes. The plants have a couple of other characteristics in common: They tend to produce lobed fruit, and they often enjoy some measure of resistance to early and late blights.

You may be able to find some heirloom plants at

local nurseries that venture beyond the obvious hybrids. But to explore this crop's great diversity, you have to begin at the beginning, with seeds. Sow them indoors six to eight weeks before the last frost date for your area. You can speed their germination by providing bottom heat and temperatures between 75 and 85 degrees F. Don't worry about giving the seedlings light until you see the first true (toothed) leaves. At that point, transplant seedlings to pots from 2 to 4 inches in diameter; the larger the pot, the sturdier the plant and the less chance of watering too much or too little. The seedlings should have cooler temperatures at this stage of their development, between 50 and 55 degrees. Cool nights and plenty of light prevent the plants from becoming spindly.

Leftover seeds remain viable for up to five years or so if stored in a cool, dry place. And you might not have to plant seed at all, if you rely on volunteer seedlings from the fringes of the compost pile. Given the heat of the composting process and nutritional benefits of the site, these plants can get off to a good start. Earl Lehman, a northern Pennsylvania gardener who also fishes and bow hunts for much of the family's food, relies on compost pile transplants to stock his tomato patch. Making use of accidental tomatoes was common practice in the 1800s. In 1866, Fearing Burr, Jr., wrote in *Garden Vegetables and How to Cultivate Them* that such plants "are generally hardy and stocky, and, when transplanted, often succeed as well, and frequently produce fruits as early, as plants from the hot-bed or nursery-bed."

If seedlings look leggy and weak when it's time to set them out, plant them more deeply in the soil; the lower stems will develop roots and anchor the plants

SKINNING TOMATOES

When tomatoes are eaten fresh, the skin tends to be all but unnoticeable. But cooking can make the skins more prominent, and many cooks prefer to remove them. There is a hot trick for doing this, and a cold one. With the hot method, you drop tomatoes, one by one, into a pot of boiling water, wait 15 seconds, then place them in cold water. The skins should split. Or, if you are storing tomatoes by freezing them whole, the skins can simply be rubbed off under the faucet in a stream of hot water. Neither trick will make easy work of removing the skins of unripe tomatoes.

more securely. Allow 1 to 2 feet between determinate plants and staked indeterminates. In the 1800s, gardeners often allowed indeterminate tomatoes to roam and set down roots—literally—along their wandering stems. But today the fashion is to use a stake or cage to save space and get the fruits off the ground. Another possible advantage is that supported plants catch more sunlight, which translates to better-flavored fruits. Garden stores sell ready-made cages, but you can save money by making your own from rolls of mesh with spacing large enough to reach through (and bring out a tomato). To keep cages from toppling, tie them to stakes driven alongside. Once plants are under way in the garden, you can increase production by pruning the vegetative shoots—those programmed to grow leaves, not tomatoes—for greater production. Look for shoots appearing between the main stem and branches. Try growing small-fruited varieties in five- or ten-gallon pots around the perimeter of a sunny porch or patio; in selecting pots, keep in mind that width counts for more than depth because tomato roots don't probe that far down.

HARVESTING

Pick tomatoes just before they become fully ripe and vulnerable to injury and pests. Store at room temperature, not in the refrigerator, for best flavor and texture. This bit of wisdom runs against tradition in some households: in the late 1800s, homemakers were instructed to serve tomatoes as cold as possible.

If your summer runs out of steam and some tomatoes haven't ripened, harvest them green before the first expected frost, wrap them in the clean newsprint used for mailing packages, and allow them to ripen indoors. Or eat them green. Unripe tomatoes at season's end needn't be thought of as the green flags of failure. In fact they once were a cash crop. Almost a century ago, Ida D. Bennett wrote in *The Vegetable Garden* that "green tomatoes are one of the most plentiful vegetables in the market" and can be "almost equal to eggplant when nicely cooked." Frying further develops the flavor of these tomatoes for which summer wasn't quite gracious enough.

Tomatoes can have a second life as one of the noblest things to come out of a kitchen—sauce. There is an awkward, even unsettling, metamorphosis as the fruits lose their identity, their symmetry, and become undifferentiated mush. And the aroma—could it be that generations of cooks have rushed to add strong-scented herbs as a culinary sort of deodorant? Hot, ripe tomatoes smell of swamp, of lobsters boiling. The steamy kitchen is not a pleasant place at this stage of sauce making.

Then, as the process continues, the atmosphere seems to brighten. There is the new, reborn scent of tomato sauce. Order has been restored through kitchen alchemy.

SAVING SEEDS

Tomatoes are self-pollinating. That is, the pollen of a blossom interacts with the egg of that blossom. This incestuous act, occurring out of sight behind the yellow wraps of the flower, ensures (with about 5% variation) that the resulting seeds will yield plants identical to the

abraham lincoln

matt's wild cherry

lone parent. There has been no interchange of genetic material between plants.

Keep an eye out for the one plant of a variety that performs best—in terms of adaptability, production, appearance, taste, or whatever characteristics are important to you. Harvest a few of the best tomatoes of this best plant when they are dead ripe, and scoop out the seeds. Place them in a jar, a can, or a food storage bag half filled with water for two days or so at room temperature. This curing process is thought to kill bacteria that might be on the seeds and pass on to the next generation.

To separate the seeds, put the pulp in a sieve and rinse with running water. Next, allow the seeds to dry thoroughly by spreading them out on paper towels in a warm area of the house. Store in a cool, dry place.

RED

Abraham Lincoln. Lincoln's commercial introduction was in 1923, and it remains one of the most popular red heirlooms among seed savers. The bright red fruits are large and meaty, with a sweet flavor that has made it a good choice for processing as tomato juice.

Costoluto Genovese. This one is as much fun to pronounce as it is to eat—unless your native tongue is Italian, in which case the name might sound as ordinary as, say, Big Boy. A native of the Italian Riviera, it does best where summers are warm. Seedlings get off to a healthy, roaring start. The lobed fruits may have a robust flavor if conditions are right. See if you detect a whiff of mint as you eat this one.

Temperate Tomatoes

Tomatoes will keep longer in the refrigerator, but at the cost of some of their precious flavor and texture. Store them at room temperature. If they can use a tad of ripening, place them on sunny windowsills.

Matt's Wild Cherry. "Like, wow!" begins the copy for this variety in the Johnny's Selected Seeds catalog. The company can be forgiven its exuberance, having introduced this tomato to the world. Matt's was discovered growing wild in the Mexican state of Hidalgo, and seeds made their way to Matt Liebman of the University of Maine, who passed them along to Johnny's. The tiny fruits are highly sweet and flavorful. Try them in salsa.

Reisentraub. This is the sort of variety that has you visiting the vines daily for a snack. Reisentraub's complex, smoky flavor makes people savor each bite for another nuance. It is a hit with backyard seed savers. The name, from the variety's native Germany, means "big bunch of grapes," a phrase descriptive of Reisentraub's heavy production. Plants do well in pots.

Stupice. Stupice is a Czech variety, brought to North America in the 1970s and on its way to being well known among gardeners. It is one of the first tomatoes to ripen, and the compact plants produce reliably. Try these tomatoes for drying or stewing.

Pink to Purple

Anna Russian. One of many promising varieties introduced from the former Soviet Union, this tomato has an intriguing heart shape that makes it stand out in the garden or on a platter of assorted heirlooms. Slices are firm and solid, and a deep red throughout. The flavor has a good balance of sweet and acid.

Brandywine. Could this be the perfect tomato? Brandywine comes as close as any, according to people

tiffen mennonite

brandywine

omar's lebanese

anna russian

eva purple ball

german johnson

cherokee purple

soldacki

who've sampled hundreds of varieties. It is something of a pop star, riding the crest of the new interest in old-time tomatoes, and may be the most widely grown heirloom variety. In their *Seed Savers Yearbook* entries, gardeners exhaust themselves doing justice to Brandywine's flavor—complex, loud, distinctively spicy, legendary, like a good wine. And, like enophiles, Brandywine lovers will sample several strains of the variety in an effort to find the ultimate. In a recent summer, Oklahoma gardener Darrell Merrell grew thirteen strains and pronounced the best was that of William Woys Weaver. Weaver, author of *Heirloom Vegetable Gardening* (Henry Holt, 1997), got his seed from a farmer in Lancaster County, Pennsylvania.

If there's little argument over the taste of Brandywine, its origins are in dispute. The standard history gives credit to Amish farmers around the Brandywine Valley of southeastern Pennsylvania, with a tip of the hat to seed saver Ben Quisenberry, who passed on his collection of a half-century to Seed Savers Exchange. But William Weaver believes Brandywine is a commercial introduction, first offered by Johnson and Stokes of Philadelphia in 1889. And now, Burpee, located outside of Philadelphia, claims credit in its recent heirloom seed catalog, saying that they brought out Brandywine under another name in 1886, only to have Johnson and Stokes grow its own seed and offer the same tomato by another name, the one that stuck.

Whatever its lineage, Brandywine needs a long time to go about its business—from 80 to 100 days. If your growing season allows, these large, deep pink fruits make a satisfying climax to the gardening year. The seed and plant catalog of the Landis Valley Museum in Lancaster, Pennsylvania, warns seed savers to avoid collecting seed of tomatoes that don't grow true to type; if Brandywine plants appear with ordinary foliage, rather than the distinctive potato leaf, pull them rather than risk cross-pollination, "which could muddy the genetic background of the plants you want to save." The catalog explains that this so-called roguing process "is a type of selection that seed savers accept as part of gardening."

Cherokee Purple. Cherokee backs up its attention-getting appearance with thin skin and exceptional sweet flavor. The plants may flag in the heat of midsummer, then begin producing again when the weather cools. The variety is said to come from Tennessee, but the connection with the Cherokee Nation seems uncertain.

Eva Purple Ball. Seeds were brought to North America from the Black Forest region of Germany in the late 1800s. The color is in fact closer to a deep pink; Carolyn J. Male, a microbiologist who co-edits *Off the Vine* newsletter, explains that "purple in tomato language means pink." Color aside, she places Eva among the best of the four hundred varieties she grows. Fruits tend to drop from the vine when ripe, so keep an eye out.

German Johnson. Mild, but not bland, is how gardeners describe this yellow-shouldered heirloom in the *Seed Savers Yearbook*. Commercial seed companies have responded to German Johnson's word-of-mouth popularity, helping to rescue it from obscurity. It is a good choice for canning.

Omar's Lebanese. Carolyn J. Male has enthusiastically disseminated free seed to her fellow seed savers. She believes the source is a hill town in Lebanon. There is a saltiness about it, as if nature had fine-tuned the taste with a shaker. The firm, meaty texture recommends Omar for sandwich slices.

Soldacki. Soldacki arrived in North America from Krakow, Poland, in the early 1900s. Expect a nice balance of sweet and tart and a considerable yield. Soldacki is a good canner.

Tiffen Mennonite. Tiffen is a potato-leafed variety producing large, good-tasting fruits with an agreeable skunky scent. It is quite similar to Brandywine. The variety is said to have been grown by Mennonite communities around the north central Ohio town of Tiffen.

YELLOW TO ORANGE

Azoychka. These golden globes are as glorious as any sight in the garden. The fruits may be bland and cry out for salt, but some growers report a citrusy flavor. Slices tend to be rather watery. Azoychka was recently collected by Seed Savers Exchange from an elderly seed seller at a market in Moscow.

Djena Lee's Golden Girl. The fruits have excellent flavor and a meaty texture. This is a family heirloom from Minnesota, dating from 1929 and named for the woman who fostered it.

Golden Queen. This handsome variety is sweet and low in acid, as you might expect (but don't always get) from a yellow tomato. Look for a pink blush on the bottom of the smooth, waxy fruits. Golden Queen had its commercial debut in Livingston's catalog for 1882.

Hugh's. Hugh's is sweet and mild, its tender skin hardly noticeable. The variety came from Madison County, Indiana, around 1940. Illinois gardener Merlyn Neidens finds that the big, pale fruits, weighing up to two pounds, draw repeat customers to his farmers' market stand.

Russian Persimmon. This variety was brought to North America by Seed Savers Exchange and is named for its vivid hue. It is sweet and mild, but may have more tartness than most yellow or orange tomatoes. Plants are stocky and don't need tall cages.

Striped German. This variety yields big, impressive fruits, waxy and beautiful. When sliced, they reveal a red pattern hidden within. The flavor is very good but in some summers may be too mild for you if your preference is for a full-bore tomato.

Verna Orange. The fruits are distinctive on the bush and on the plate—when sliced, Verna Orange reveals a nearly solid interior, something like a muskmelon. The taste, too, seems to be akin to a melon, or is that the power of visual suggestion? This heirloom comes from Indiana.

Yellow Pear. As with other old-time nonred tomatoes, Yellow Pear was once considered a pretty novelty rather than a proper vegetable. Another strike against it was small size; cherry-size tomatoes were relegated to the pickling jar.

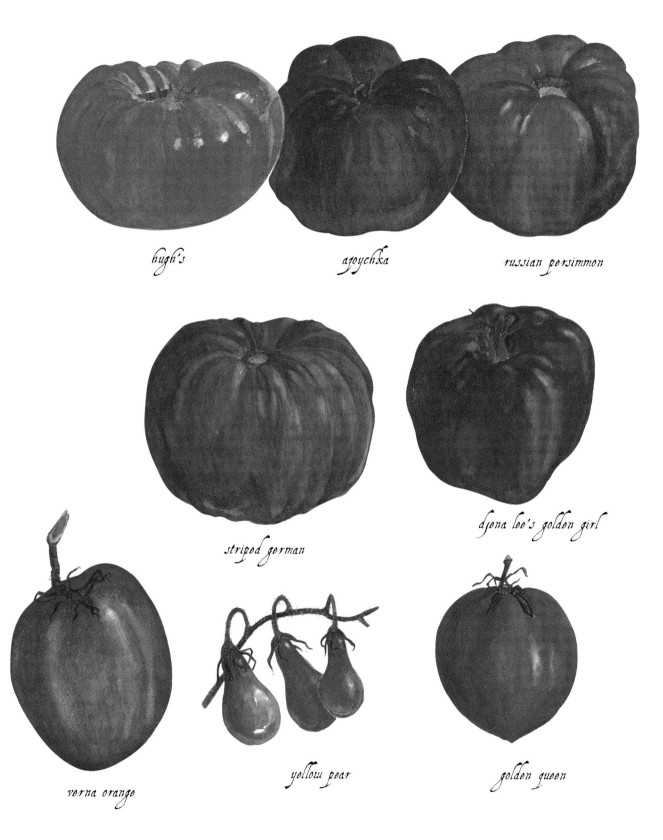

hugh's

azoychka

russian persimmon

striped german

djena lee's golden girl

verna orange

yellow pear

golden queen

And yet, today, Yellow Pear is found in more seed catalogs than any other yellow or orange open-pollinated variety. This must be due in part to the packaging—an unusual shape and bright color—because the fruits are sweet but not particularly rich in tomato flavor. They are suited to pies and preserves, and as a diversion in tossed salads. The clusters of bright yellow last into fall, providing one of the last cheery sights in the tomato rows.

OTHER COLORS

Aunt Ruby's German Green. Green tomato varieties, like apples that are still green when ripe, confound expectations. The eyes tell the tongue that mediocrity lies ahead—poor texture, unbalanced acidity. Aunt Ruby's is in fact a great-tasting tomato, characterized by a rich, almost skunky spiciness with a hint of smoke. Alma Weaver, a Pennsylvania market gardener, finds that Aunt Ruby's makes an excellent varietal tomato butter. Its character also comes through when juiced. The tomato isn't entirely green: Distinctive warm lines radiate from the base, as shown here. This relatively recent heirloom was named for Ruby Arnold of Tennessee.

Black Krim. With its gothic coloring, Krim wouldn't be a produce department manager's dream, but it ranks among the most commonly shared tomatoes in the *Seed Savers Yearbook*. Krim is a memorably full-flavored variety, with a hint of saltiness. It originated near the Black Sea.

THE TOMATO HERBS

Tomatoes come close to being a stand-alone vegetable—no condiments or herbs needed. And yet the near perfection of the vine-ripened fruit can be enhanced with basil or arugula. Both are easy to grow. And although basil crumples with the first breath of frost, arugula will shoulder on through cold weather. Harvest arugula leaves young and keep plants well watered to prevent the nutty flavor from being overwhelmed by a hot edge.

Black Plum. One of the most distinctive-looking varieties, Black Plum was brought to North America from Russia. The texture is meaty, and the fruits cook down into a good sauce.

Black Sea Man. Here is a third so-called black tomato from the former Soviet Union. Once you get past the oddly discolored appearance, the flavor is full and complex. Like a good wine, Black Sea Man has the palate and nose searching for nuances—melon and lemon, perhaps. This variety has yet to appear in a commercial catalog, but if you're after a good-tasting novelty, look up a gardener offering it in *Seed Savers Yearbook*.

Dr. Carolyn. If you like that characteristic burst of flavor found in some cherry tomatoes, try this delicious thin-skinned variety. It isn't an heirloom, but a recently developed mutant of Galinas, a dark yellow cherry tomato. The name honors Dr. Carolyn Male, a microbiologist and tomato enthusiast who introduced it through her *Off the Vine* newsletter.

Evergreen. Green tomato varieties suffer the same prejudice as green apples. It took Americans years to warm up to the grass-hued Granny Smith, and you aren't likely to see green tomatoes outside of backyard gardens and roadside stands for some time to come. Evergreen indicates that it is ready to be harvested when the fruits take on a golden glow. Don't allow them to languish on the vine, because Evergreen's flavor goes away when the tomatoes are overripe. Try using it in green salsas and as a ripe alternative for fried green tomatoes. The flavor is complex, suggesting mint and smoke—nothing whatsoever like that of an unripe fruit.

Green Grape. This fruit looks more like a large green olive than either a grape or a tomato, making it a conversation piece for the hors d'oeuvre tray or salad bowl. But Green Grape is more than a novelty; it has a good texture and interesting flavor. It is the descendent of heirlooms rather than an antique itself, having been bred by crossing Evergreen and Yellow Pear.

Green Zebra. Beneath the striking exterior lies an excellent, sweet-tart flavor. Green Zebra is ready to be picked when the stripes show clearly. Jerry Moomaw of Glouster, Ohio, says Green Zebra is the most popular tomato he offers at his market stand.

Schimmeig Striped Hollow. This orange-streaked red tomato is indeed hollow. It feels light in the hand and when opened looks similar to a bell pepper. The taste is rather bland, but Schimmeig's talent is that it can be stuffed with a flavorful filling.

White Wonder. The color seems suggestive of both mystery and blandness, but in fact this variety is firm and has the good, cheery flavor you'd expect to find in a red tomato.

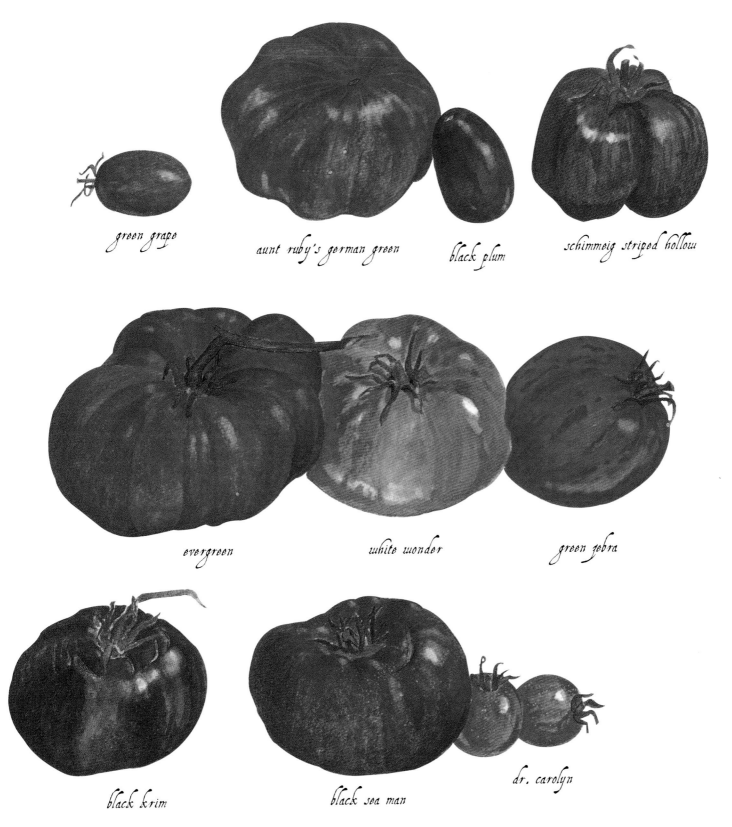

green grape

aunt ruby's german green

black plum

schimmeig striped hollow

evergreen

white wonder

green zebra

black krim

black sea man

dr. carolyn

Tomato on a Bagel

This bagel sandwich barely qualifies as a recipe, but it is included here as a reminder that tomatoes are best enjoyed right off the vine, with the sun's heat still in them. Unlike certain other vegetables, they don't need elaborate procedures or a list of supporting ingredients to be delightful. No utensils, no seasoning—although some gardeners visit their tomato rows with a salt shaker in a back pocket. As scripted here, this is a sense-tickling mess of a sandwich. Tuck a napkin in your collar.

Have a jar of mayonnaise, butter, salt, and torn leaves of cilantro, arugula, or basil at the ready. Go out into the garden and harvest the biggest, most perfectly ripened tomato you can find. Back in the kitchen, cut 2 generous slices from the middle for the sandwich. Cut a bagel in half and toast it, cut sides down, in a dry frying pan over medium heat. When the bagel is just turning golden, promptly butter the cut sides, put a slice of tomato on each, slather the sides with mayonnaise, administer a shake of salt, and crown with the leaves. Eat at once.

Unadorned Tomato Sauce

Many gardeners prefer their tomato sauce in its simplest form, rather than freight it with the darling ingredient of the moment. By paring ingredients down to the basics, you allow the tomatoes you've grown to speak their quiet varietal voices.

Any tomato can be made into sauce, but you should expect to simmer off more liquid from those not known as good sauce and paste producers.

Remove the skins and soften the tomatoes by placing them in boiling water for 2 or 3 minutes. Remove them with a slotted spoon to a colander, run cold water over them, and peel the skins. Cut out the stem end and any blemished areas. Hold the tomato over the pan in which you will be making sauce and cut off thin pieces to make a smoother consistency. The pan catches everything from this messy process, and keeps the kitchen a little tidier.

Simmer over low heat, uncovered, stirring occasionally. Sauce day will go more quickly if you put all the burners to work, each with its burbling pan. Cook until you arrive at the consistency you want. For a smoother sauce, set it aside to cool somewhat, then pass it through a food mill or puree briefly in a blender. Refrigerate sauce that you intend to use within a few days. Freeze or hot-pack the rest in jars.

TOMATO BUTTER

MAKES ABOUT 2 PINTS

This recipe calls itself a butter because ketchup has become a debased, humdrum condiment with nothing remarkable but its shelf life. The nineteenth century was ketchup's golden age. People brewed their own at home, using such ingredients as brandy, white wine, peach leaves, flowers, and seaweed. Then commercial producers brought out the sugary version we know today, and ketchup recipes gradually disappeared from cookbooks.

This butter is dark and rich. It can be spooned over anything from breakfast grits to a before-bed dish of ice cream. You'll get a thicker product using fewer tomatoes and less time if you use a sauce variety, but this recipe will work with anything that happens to be ripe.

1 onion, finely chopped
2 tablespoons olive oil
5 pounds tomatoes, skinned (see page 165) and chopped

¼ cup (packed) brown sugar
1 cup red wine vinegar
¼ cup sweet vermouth
1 teaspoon salt

Sauté the onion in the oil in a large skillet; the wider the cooking vessel, the sooner the butter will steam off its excess liquid. Stir in all the other ingredients and simmer, uncovered, for about 1 hour or until the butter has reached a good thick consistency. (For a smoother butter, interrupt the simmering, let the mixture cool, and pass it through a food mill or puree it in a blender or food processor. Return to the heat.) Begin with medium heat and lower the temperature as the butter thickens, to prevent scorching. Refrigerate as much as you think you'll use in a couple of weeks and freeze or can the rest.

FRESH TOMATO SAUCE

SERVES 4

*Yes, making your own slow-simmered tomato sauce is worth
all the straining, stirring, and steam.*

4 to 6 medium to large tomatoes,
  chopped
2 tablespoons finely chopped basil
3 tablespoons olive oil
1 tablespoon red wine vinegar

½ teaspoon salt
½ teaspoon ground black pepper
Hot cooked pasta
Grated parmigiano or romano
  cheese (optional)

Place the tomatoes, basil, olive oil, vinegar, salt, and pepper in a bowl and stir well.
Serve the pasta with the sauce spooned over the top. Pass around a dish of grated
cheese if you'd like.

GAZPACHO

SERVES 4

*You can't get any closer to your garden than sipping a bowl of these raw,
atomized vegetables. Raw, that is, except for the first three ingredients. They're
sautéed so that they won't overpower the less-assertive ingredients.*

1 small sweet onion, quartered
2 cloves garlic, minced
1 red bell pepper, sliced
¼ cup olive oil
4 large tomatoes, skinned
  (see page 165) and chopped
1 carrot, grated
1 cucumber, peeled, seeded, and
  grated
¼ cup mixed chopped parsley, basil,
  cilantro, and arugula, as available

¼ cup red wine vinegar
¼ cup lemon juice
10 olives, pitted and slivered
1 teaspoon hot pepper sauce
1 teaspoon salt
½ teaspoon ground black pepper
1½ cups cubed day-old crusty
  white bread
Whole herb leaves, for garnish
Yogurt or sour cream, for garnish
  (optional)

Sauté the onion, garlic, and pepper in the oil until softened, about 5 minutes. Scrape into a food processor or blender, add all remaining ingredients except the garnish, and blend until smooth. Refrigerate for at least 2 hours before serving. Top each bowl with the garnish and, if you'd like, a spoonful of yogurt or sour cream.

GREEN TOMATO AND PEAR CHUTNEY

MAKES ABOUT 1 ¾ PINTS

This sounds like an odd couple to cook up into a chutney, but as summer turns into fall you may find yourself with a surfeit of both ripe pears and unripe tomatoes. Tomatoes are often used to make chutneys in India, and pears contribute something of the fruitiness of two traditional chutney staples that probably won't flourish in your garden, mangoes and tamarinds.

1 tablespoon olive oil

1 medium onion

1 teaspoon mustard seeds

2½ cups skinned (see page 165) and chopped green tomatoes

2½ cups peeled and chopped pears

½ cup raisins

¼ cup (packed) brown sugar

2 tablespoons molasses or maple syrup

½ cup red wine vinegar

2 tablespoons freshly grated ginger

1 teaspoon hot sauce

1 teaspoon ground cumin

1 teaspoon salt

Heat a skillet, add the oil, and sauté the onions until translucent, about 5 minutes. Push them to the side and heat the mustard seeds in the cleared area until they start to pop. Add the remaining ingredients, stir in well, and simmer for 30 minutes, stirring occasionally to prevent sticking. Cover only if the chutney reaches the right consistency before the tomatoes and pears are tender. Refrigerate as much as you think you'll use in a couple of weeks and freeze or can the rest.

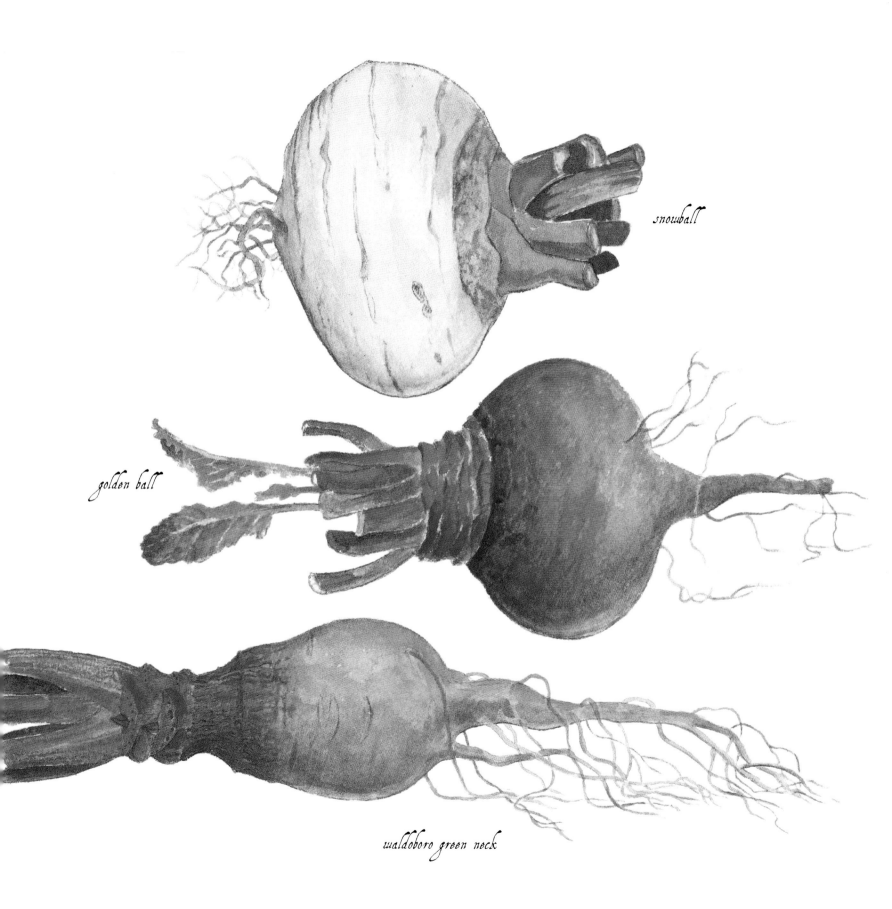

snowball

golden ball

waldoboro green neck

The turnip has been typecast as a frowsy accompaniment to enormous platters of meat. And that's all the attention it deserves when reduced by overcooking to watery cubes tasting vaguely of melted snow. Served in this way, turnips seem to beg to become extinct. It doesn't come as a complete surprise, then, that between 1981 and 1994

TURNIPS

the number of open-pollinated turnip varieties offered by seed companies dropped by more than a third, according to Seed Saver Publications.

But a fresh turnip, harvested small, is a delight. Some are pretty, and a couple are even stunning. All benefit from sympathetic treatment in the kitchen. Young turnips can be julienned for crudités. Grated turnips are especially sweet when sautéed quickly. And steamed turnips maintain their firmness and flavor. The tops are an overlooked resource. They taste like a trendier vegetable, broccoli rabe, which in fact happens to be a close relative. A few turnip varieties are grown specifically for their greens.

GROWING

Turnips are not a great challenge to grow if the soil is reasonably loose and friable so that the roots can expand. Plant in early spring and again at the end of summer: The dog days are not turnip weather. Sow seeds 1 inch apart and ¼ to ½ inch deep, in rows spaced every 12 to 18 inches. Thin to 4 inches apart within rows and steam the seedlings as spring greens.

HARVESTING

The first small turnips may be ready to enjoy just a month after sowing. It's common practice to peel turnips, but if you harvest them young—from 2 to 3 inches in diameter—you may be able to skip this step with most varieties. Bring in turnips before hard frosts unless you protect them with mulch.

SAVING SEEDS

To keep turnips from cross-pollinating with their own kind, as well as with mustard and Chinese cabbage, plants should be isolated at least 200 feet, up to a quarter mile for best insurance.

VARIETIES

Gilfeather. Gardeners like this turnip for its mild, sweet flavor and creamy texture when cooked and mashed. Roots grow quite large without developing a woody, flavorless core. It was developed by a Vermont farmer, John Gilfeather, in the late 1800s. Pennsylvania gardener Donna Irwin, who grew the model for the illustration, says that after tasting Gilfeather, "you'll never eat Purple-Tops again."

Golden Ball. This 1859 heirloom is sweeter and milder than the commonly grown Purple-Top White Globe. Sunlight turns the tops green, and Arkansas seed seller Blane Bourgeois grows this variety close together so that the plants make their own shade and remain pale.

Purple-Top White Globe. When freshly exhumed, this variety is as brilliant as any above-ground vegetable, its clean white globe blushed with magenta from exposure to sunlight. Purple-Top is the familiar turnip of both supermarkets and roadside stands. Having been grown for more than a century, it is one of the most durably popular of heirlooms. Appearance must have something to do with that, but so does taste. Purple-Tops are especially tender when harvested young. The greens are good steamed or sautéed.

Scarlet Ball. A beautiful, mild heirloom from Japan, Scarlet Ball looks more like a beet; even the foliage has red veins. As the roots are cooked, the flesh is tinged by the skin.

Snowball. Once known less prettily as Early Six Weeks, Snowball is a summer turnip with a crisp, tender texture and a pure white globe. Arkansas grower Blane Bourgeois, who offers more than three hundred varieties through Seed Savers Exchange, grates this and other mild turnips to make a sort of coleslaw, without cooking.

Waldoboro Green Neck. Folklore has it that this variety drifted to the Maine coast when a ship foundered off shore. Waldoboro Green Neck dates back to Revolutionary days and takes its name from a Maine town where it was grown. Quality remains good even if the roots are allowed to grow large.

scarlet ball

gilfeather

purple-top white globe

HOT TURNIP SNACK

*Turnips as a snack food? Yes, and if you have children whose
interest in vegetables stops at ketchup, try grating up a pile of turnips for an
after-school treat on a cool fall day. Serve with a glass of cider.*

4 small to medium turnips, grated   ¼ cup grated cheese (any type)
2 tablespoons olive oil   Balsamic vinegar

Heat the oil in a skillet and add the turnips along with 1 or 2 tablespoons water.
Cover and cook, turning the turnips occasionally with a spatula to ensure even
cooking, for about 5 minutes. Turn off the heat, sprinkle the vinegar and cheese over
the top, and put the lid back on for 1 minute. Serve hot.

🖉 *Turnips are also used in Parsnip Tagine (page 103) and Minted Peas in Turnip Cups
(page 108). Turnip greens can be used in Chard Calzones (page 53), Chard Frittata
(page 52), and Hortopita (page 95).*

SOURCES

SEEDS

Abundant Life Seed Foundation
PO Box 772
Port Townsend, WA 98368
An impressive range of beans, corn, lettuce, winter squash, and tomatoes. The company takes the trouble to name and thank the growers who supply it with seeds.

Boone's Native Seed Co.
PO Box 10363
Raleigh, NC 27605
A selective offering of tomatoes and peppers.

Bountiful Garden Seeds
18001 Shafer Ranch Road
Willits, CA 95490
A large and interesting selection of seeds, all of them open-pollinated and untreated and some labeled as organically grown. Computer-printed labels on each seed packet give explicit planting directions, meaning fewer muddy fingerprints in your gardening books.

W. Atlee Burpee
300 Park Avenue
Warminster, PA 18974
In addition to its general catalog, Burpee publishes one devoted to heirloom vegetables and flowers and illustrated with period illustrations.

Comstock, Ferre & Co.
263 Main Street
Wethersfield, CT 06109

The Cook's Garden
PO Box 535
Londonderry, VT 05148
One of the best catalogs in terms of both selection and vegetable descriptions.

Deep Diversity
PO Box 15189
Santa Fe, NM 87506
Carries more than 100 varieties not available through other catalogs.

Down on the Farm Seed
PO Box 184
Hiram, OH 44234

Evergreen Y.H. Enterprises
PO Box 17538
Anaheim, CA 92817
An excellent selection of East Asian vegetables.

Filaree Farm
182 Conconully Highway
Okanogan, WA 98840
An astonishing number of garlic varieties.

Fisher's Seeds
PO Box 236
20750 East Frontage Street
Belgrade, MT 59714
An old family company, noting the best choices for that region's high altitudes and short growing seasons.

Fox Hollow Seed Co.
PO Box 148
McGrann, PA 16236
A good selection of heirloom varieties, available in low-cost "sample packs."

Garden City Seeds
778 Highway 93 North
Hamilton, MT 59840
The catalog's growing information is particularly helpful.

Gaze Seed Co. Ltd.
PO Box 640
9 Buchanan Street
St. John's, Newfoundland A1C 5K8
Canada
Vegetable varieties chosen with the Newfoundland climate in mind.

Grandview Farms Tomato Seeds
12942 Dupont Road
Sebastopol, CA 95472
An extensive list of open-pollinated varieties.

Heirloom Seed Project
Landis Valley Museum
2451 Kissel Hill Road
Lancaster, PA 17601
An unusual selection of seeds, including many varieties traditionally grown by the Pennsylvania Dutch.

Heirloom Seeds
PO Box 245
West Elizabeth, PA 15088-0245

Heritage Seed Co.
PO Box 505
Star City, AR 71667-0505
Offerings feature garlic and onions.

Horticultural Enterprises
PO Box 810082
Dallas, TX 75381-0082
The company's motto reads, "Happiness is staying healthy eating chiles," and its flyer lists a good selection of varieties.

Horus Botanicals
HCR Route 82
PO Box 29
Salem, AR 72576
*An eclectic listing favoring okra,
garlic, Asian greens, peppers,
eggplants, tomatoes, and beans.*

Howe Sound Seeds
PO Box 109
Bowen Island,
British Columbia V0N 1G0
Canada
*A small selection of vegetable varieties
grown in the late-Victorian period.*

Johnny's Selected Seeds
310 Foss Hill Road
Albion, ME 04910-9731
*The catalog is among the most useful, with
its unusually detailed growing information.
Johnny's takes an active role in
encouraging gardeners to save their own
seed and help preserve rare varieties.*

D. Landreth Seed Co.
PO Box 6426
Baltimore, MD 21230
*Landreth proclaims itself America's oldest
seed company and counts George
Washington and Thomas Jefferson among
its past customers. The catalog notes that
Landreth had been in business 36 years
before it offered tomatoes, because of their
lingering reputation as a poisonous
ornamental.*

Le Jardin du Gourmet
PO Box 75
St. Johnsbury Center, VT 05863-0075
*A source for shallots and an interesting
selection of vegetable seeds emphasizing
endives, leeks, and mâche.*

Mapel Seeds
PO Box 551
North Grafton, MA 01536

Native Seeds/SEARCH
2509 North Campbell Avenue #325
Tucson, AZ 85719
*Published by a nonprofit group, the
catalog offers an unequaled selection of
varieties grown by native peoples of the
southwestern United States and northern
Mexico, especially beans (including wild
varieties), peas, chilies, corn, and squash.
According to Seed Saver Publications,
this catalog offers more unique varieties—
that is, selections carried by no other
mail-order source—than any other. Free
seed is offered to Native Americans
living in the region.*

Old Sturbridge Village
Sturbridge, MA 01566
A small sampling of heirloom vegetables.

Pepper Gal
PO Box 23006
Ft. Lauderdale, FL 33307
*A fount of hot pepper varieties, some 50
of which aren't available in other
commercial catalogs.*

Peters Seed and Research
407 Marantha Lane
Myrtle Creek, OR 97457
*Introduces varieties from its own breeding
program.*

Pinetree Garden Seeds
PO Box 300
New Gloucester, ME 04260

Prairie Grown Garden Seeds
PO Box 118
Cochin, Saskatchewan S0M 0L0
Canada
*In this chatty catalog, owner Jim Ternier
says he's a bit short on a couple of varieties
and offers to swap seeds with anyone who
has a surplus. He describes having to
shovel a foot of show in order to harvest
the last of his beans and radishes.*

Ronninger's Seed Potatoes
Star Route
Moyie Springs, ID 83845
*The biggest offering of naturally
grown seed potatoes in the
United States.*

Salt Spring Seeds
PO Box 444
Ganges
Salt Spring Island,
British Columbia V8K 2W1
Canada
*Vegetables suited to northern climates,
as well as an impressive number
of dry bean varieties.*

Sand Hill Preservation Center
1878 230th Street
Calamus, IO 52729
*The catalog lists both heirloom vegetables
and heirloom poultry (among the chickens
is "Blue Old English—slim, feisty in
temperament"). The list is particularly
strong in tomatoes and sweet potatoes.*

Seeds Blüm
HC 33 Idaho City Stage
Boise, ID 83706
*A fascinating, rambling, unpredictable
catalog, rich in potatoes and out-of-the-
ordinary vegetables.*

Seeds of Change
PO Box 15700
Santa Fe, NM 87506
*One of the standard sources for heirlooms,
with a focus on varieties for the
Southwest. The catalog's color photography
is excellent.*

Shepherd's Garden Seeds
30 Irene Steet
Torrington, CT 06790
*An excellent selection of heirlooms, with
generous descriptions of each. Includes
many European varieties.*

R. H. Shumway
PO Box 1
Graniteville, SC 29829

Sourcepoint Organic Seeds
1647 2725 Road
Cedaredge, CO 81413
Many unusual open-pollinated varieties, listed in the catalog by Latin names.

Southern Exposure Seed Exchange
PO Box 170
Earlysville, VA 22936
An impressive selection of heirloom seeds, much of them grown by the company itself—not standard practice, as some seed houses are only distributors of seed produced elsewhere. The catalog discusses the trade-offs between open-pollinated and hybrid varieties, seed saving, and heirlooms.

Synergy Seeds
PO Box 323
Orleans, CA 95556
A price list strong on beans and tomatoes.

Terra Edibles
PO Box 63
Foxboro, Ontario K0K 3H0
Canada
An informal catalog offering unusual varieties, with occasional notes on the best selections for Canadian growers.

Territorial Seed Company
PO Box 157
Cottage Grove, OR 97424
A highly informative catalog, and of particular interest to short-season gardeners.

Thomas Jefferson Center for Historic Plants
Monticello
PO Box 316
Charlottesville, VA 22902
Heirloom vegetables and flowers, some of which were grown by Jefferson.

Tomato Growers Supply Company
PO Box 2237
Fort Myers, FL 33902
An extensive selection of tomatoes and peppers, including many heirlooms. The catalog gives clear, detailed growing information.

Underwood Gardens
4N381 Maple Avenue
Bensenville, IL 60106

Willhite Seed, Inc.
PO Box 23
Poolville, TX 76487
Offers many cantaloupes and watermelons.

Stanley Zubrowski
PO Box 26
Prairie River, Saskatchewan S0E 1J0
Canada
A typed list of tomato varieties.

Books

Ausubel, Kenny. *Seeds of Change.* San Francisco: Harper San Francisco, 1994.

Bubel, Nancy. *The New Seed-Starters Handbook.* Emmaus, PA: Rodale Press, 1988.

Burr, Jr., Fearing. *The Field and Garden Vegetables of America.* Chillicothe, IL: The American Botanist, 1988. Reprint of 1865 edition.

_____. *Garden Vegetables and How to Cultivate Them.* Boston: J.E. Tilton, 1866.

Deppe, Carol. *Breed Your Own Vegetable Varieties.* Boston: Little, Brown, 1993.

Garden Seed Inventory. Decorah, IA: Seed Saver Publications, 1995 (published annually).

Henderson, Peter. *Henderson's Handbook of Plants.* New York: Peter Henderson, 1890.

Jabs, Carolyn. *The Heirloom Gardener.* San Francisco: Sierra Club Books, 1984.

Phillips, Roger, and Martyn Rix. *Vegetables.* New York: Random House, 1993.

Seed Savers 1997 Yearbook. Decorah, IA: Seed Saver Publications, 1997 (published annually).

Watson, Benjamin. *Taylor's Guide to Heirloom Vegetables.* Boston: Houghton Mifflin, 1996.

Weaver, William Woys. *Heirloom Vegetable Gardening.* New York: Henry Holt, 1997.

Whealy, Kent, and Steve Demuth. *Fruit, Berry and Nut Inventory.* Decorah, IA: Seed Saver Publications, 1993.

Periodicals

Off the Vine
Carolyn J. Male,
21-2 Latham Village Lane
Latham, NY 12110
A chatty newsletter devoted to tomatoes and larger heirloom topics, with occasional free offers to subscribers of free seed from experimental crosses.

Tomato Club Newsletter
PO Box 418
Bogota, NJ 07603-0418
Out of print as of 1997, but back issues are available.

ORGANIZATIONS

CORNS
c/o Carl L. and Karen D. Barnes
Route 1, Box 32
Turpin, OK 73950

Garden Research Exchange
61 South Bartlett Street
Kingston, Ontario K7K 1X3
Canada

Joseph Schneider House
Heritage Seed Program
466 Queen Street South
Kitchener, Ontario N2G 1W7
Canada

**Medomak Valley High School Heirloom
Seed Project**
Manktown Road
Waldoboro, ME 04572

Seed Savers Exchange
3076 North Winn Road
Decorah, IA 52101
Publishes Garden Seed Inventory, *as
well as the annual* Seed Savers Yearbook
and Flower and Herb Exchange.

Seeds of Diversity Canada
PO Box 36, Station Q
Toronto, Ontario M4T 2C7
Canada

ACKNOWLEDGMENTS

To the extent that the watercolors in this book manage to fool your eye, credit goes to the teaching of Liz Osborne at the Pennsylvania Academy of the Fine Arts and Myron Barnstone at Barnstone Studios.

Ali Nass-Yepsen tinkered with many of the recipes and came up with several of her own. Among those who supplied recipes or the inspiration behind them were Sue Gronholz; Sharon Koury; Donna Irwin; Stephen D. Posey; Dorothy Beiswenger; Lois Dunton; Susan Derecskey; George Sfetsios; Bill Rogers; Michael Gambill; Tom Paetzell; August F. Schuman; François Choveau; Michael Geary, chef of the Farmhouse Restaurant in Emmaus, Pennsylvania; my brother Carter Yepsen and, through him, Podere le Rose language and cooking school in Tuscany, Italy; and my father and mother, Roger and Natalie Yepsen. Several seed merchants were generous with recipes: R. F. Boone of Boone's Native Seed Co.; Fox Hollow Seed Co.; Fred's Plant Farm; Native Seeds/SEARCH; Valerie Phipps at Phipps Bean Ranch; and Robson Farms.

Most of the vegetables illustrated here were grown in the author's Pennsylvania garden. Others were provided by James Weaver; Richard Prince; Donna Irwin; Clyde Conaway; William Woys Weaver; Larime Wilson of Wylie House Museum, Bloomington, Indiana; George G. Darby; Phyllis and James Wolfe; Wayne L. Jeidy; Douglas Hendrickson; Blane Bourgeois of Horus Botanicals, Salem, Arkansas; and Will Bonsall of the Scatterseed Project, Farmington, Maine. Thanks also to Peter Strauss, James Weaver, Jack Ruttle, Bob and Cindy Seip, Earl Lehman, Tim Stark, Barb Fritz, and dozens of Seed Saver Exchange members for talking shop.

INDEX